More Advance Praise for
Emotional Intelligence for Sales Success

"*Emotional Intelligence for Sales Success* is a must-read for selling in today's environment. This book will strike a cord with anyone in sales looking for an edge in the marketplace. Colleen shows her depth of experience in EI selling, and delivers compelling insight that is invaluable to building a sales organization that truly will capture and drive results not only in the present but for many prosperous years to come!"
— Spencer Warren, VP of Sales, U.S. Foods, Denver, Colorado

"Before you make another sales call, read Colleen's book. *Emotional Intelligence for Sales Success* is extremely readable, provocative, yet practical. Anyone selling anything can benefit from her research, experience, and proven strategies."
— Jane Applegate, author of *201 Great Ideas for Your Small Business*; and Executive Producer SmallBizWorldTV.com

"*Emotional Intelligence for Sales Success* is a dramatic departure from the vast majority of sales books. The critical importance that Emotional Intelligence plays in the sales process is not well understood and seldom taught. Colleen Stanley offers a clear step-by-step guide with real-world examples that will help all salespeople understand and apply these difference-making concepts. This is an essential read for all salespeople and sales leaders."
— David Sass, VP and General Manager, North American Corporation

"This book is an engaging guide to incorporating the principles of Emotional Intelligence into your arsenal of selling skills. I highly recommend it for any individual or organization that is looking to attain the next level of success."
— Kirk Schreck, COO, ServiceMagic, Denver, Colorado

Emotional Intelligence for Sales Success

Connect with Customers and Get Results

Colleen Stanley

⋌AMACOM

American Management Association

New York • Atlanta • Brussels • Chicago • Mexico City • San Francisco
Shanghai • Tokyo • Toronto • Washington, D.C.

Bulk discounts available. For details visit:
www.amacombooks.org/go/specialsales
Or contact special sales:
Phone: 800-250-5308
Email: specialsls@amanet.org
View all the AMACOM titles at: www.amacombooks.org
American Management Association: www.amanet.org

This publication is designed to provide accurate and authoritative information in regard to the subject matter covered. It is sold with the understanding that the publisher is not engaged in rendering legal, accounting, or other professional service. If legal advice or other expert assistance is required, the services of a competent professional person should be sought.

Library of Congress Cataloging-in-Publication Data

Stanley, Colleen.
    Emotional intelligence for sales success : connect with customers and get results / Colleen Stanley.
        p.   cm.
    Includes bibliographical references and index.
    ISBN-13: 978-0-8144-3029-3
    ISBN-10: 0-8144-3029-5
        1. Selling—Psychological aspects.   2. Customer relations—Psychological aspects.
    3. Emotional intelligence.   I. Title.

    HF5438.8.P75S73 2013
    658.8501'9—dc23

                                                                                2012016589

About AMA
American Management Association (www.amanet.org) is a world leader in talent development, advancing the skills of individuals to drive business success. Our mission is to support the goals of individuals and organizations through a complete range of products and services, including classroom and virtual seminars, webcasts, webinars, podcasts, conferences, corporate and government solutions, business books and research. AMA's approach to improving performance combines experiential learning—learning through doing—with opportunities for ongoing professional growth at every step of one's career journey.

Printing number
10   9   8   7

This book is dedicated to our wonderful clients. Thank you for making work such a pleasure. Thanks to my husband, Jim. Your unconditional support continues to amaze me.

Contents

Foreward by Jill Konrath   xi

Introduction   xiii

Part I   The What, Why, and How of
         Emotional Intelligence and
         Sales Results

Chapter 1   Closing the Knowing-and-Doing Gap:
             When You Know Better, You Do Better   3

    Understanding Emotional Intelligence   4
    Emotional Intelligence and Sales Results   7
    The Business Case for "Return on Emotions"   10
    Action Steps for Improving Your Emotional
        Intelligence   14

Chapter 2   The Art and Neuroscience of Sales:
             The New Way to Influence   21

    Selling to the Old Brain   22
    The Emotionally Intelligent Response   27
    Walk a Mile in Your Prospect's Shoes   30
    Putting It All Together   34
    Action Steps for Improving Your Ability to Influence   35

Part II   Emotional Intelligence and the Sales Process

Chapter 3   Prospecting:
                  The Real Reason for
                  Empty Sales Pipelines   43

Are You a Sales Marshmallow Grabber?   44

Drive-By Relationships   51

Sales Reality Check   54

Are You Stressed Out?   56

The Neuroscience of Prospecting   58

Action Steps for Improving Your Prospecting Results   60

Chapter 4   Likeability:
                  All Things Being Equal, People
                  Buy from People They Like   67

Would You Buy from You?   69

It's All About *Them*: The Prospect and Customer   72

Know, Relate, and Build Likeability   77

Are You Showing Up or Living It Up?   80

Are You a Joy Giver?   82

Action Steps for Improving Your Likeability   84

Chapter 5   Expectations:
                  You Get What You Expect   87

Partnership or Vendor-ship?   89

What's Your Mindset?   90

Set and Manage Expectations to Create Raving Fans   98

Action Steps for Improving the Way You
      Manage Expectations   100

Chapter 6   Questioning Skills:
             What's Your Prospect's Story?   105

Listen Before You Leap   107
Use the "3Ws" Formula   108
Make Your Prospect's Brain Hurt   111
Get to the Real Pain   112
Determine the Commitment to Change   114
Agree and Align   116
Action Steps for Improving Your Questioning
    Skills   119

Chapter 7   Reaching Decision Makers:
             *How to Better Connect
             and Meet*   122

How People Make Decisions   124
Are You Meeting with Mr. No?   134
Are You Asking the Right Question?   136
Action Steps for Improving Your Ability to
    Reach Decision Makers   138

Chapter 8   Checkbook:
             Get Paid What You Are Worth   142

What Is Your "Money Talk"?   145
Learn to Deal with Good Negotiators   148
Are You Willing to Walk?   151
Examine Your Sales Pipeline   154
Conviction and Confidence   154
Action Steps for Improving Your Ability to
    Get Paid What You Are Worth   156

Chapter 9   People Over Process:
             *The Key Traits of Emotionally
             Intelligent Sales Cultures*   160

Are You Learning or Lagging?   163

There Is No "I" in Team   168

It's Better to Give   174

Action Steps for Building Emotionally Intelligent
    Sales Cultures   176

Chapter 10   Take the Lead:
             *Sales Leadership and
             Emotional Intelligence*   179

How Do You Show Up?   180

Do Your Words and Actions Align?   182

Teaching Rather Than Closing   183

Tough Love, Sales Leadership Style   186

The Most Overlooked Motivator of Them All   191

Best Practices for Sales Leadership   192

Action Steps for Improving Your Emotional
    Intelligence in Sales Leadership   194

Index   199

Foreword

WHAT DOES A MARSHMALLOW EXPERIMENT have to do with sales success? That's exactly what I wondered when Colleen Stanley started talking at the sales conference about a study where kids were told they could have one marshmallow now or two if they'd wait a few minutes.

As it turns out, their ability to delay immediate gratification had a huge impact on their success in school. And, as Colleen explained, salespeople who avoid premature closing succeed much more often than those who can't.

Whoa! I thought. This lady is onto something. Then, when she started talking about the multiple aspects of emotional intelligence (EI), I knew she'd found the "missing link."

Salespeople with low EI frequently sabotage themselves, even after the best sales training in the world. At the same time, their peers with both high intrapersonal and interpersonal EI consistently outperform others.

Turns out that these "soft skills," which have so long been pooh-poohed by the business community, are much more than just warm fuzzies. Instead of being of little consequence, they're big-time significant.

Recently I spoke to a group of talented young sales professionals. Real go-getters. They had a track record of success prior to getting the job at this high growth company. The CEO asked me to speak about my early years in sales—something I hadn't thought about for a long time.

As I reflected on my first sales job at Xerox, I was amazed at the emotion that kept popping into my mind—*fear!* To start with, I was afraid I wouldn't make it in sales. Then, I worried about making my quota. After I'd succeeded in that, I feared that I couldn't replicate the success monthly. When I was promoted into major accounts, I was concerned that what I'd learned wouldn't translate to these big companies.

When I told the young reps about my angst, every one of their heads were bobbing ever-so-slightly in agreement. They knew what I meant. They felt the fear.

I believe that my ability to deal with the fear was a key factor in my success in this profession. Fortunately, I had the skills to do it myself. Otherwise, I suspect I'd be like the many people who "try" sales and discover it just isn't for them.

But that's just one aspect of EI. Here's another: At the start of my sales career, I wasn't good at working with people who weren't like me. I thought some were dense because they just didn't get it. Others were painfully slow, anal-retentive decision makers. The demanding jerks and nonstop talkers drove me crazy too. Aargh!

I had to learn how to deal with all these different types of people. It was hard. There were times I blew it badly, but ultimately I got good at it.

That's the best part. Emotional intelligence can be learned. In *Emotional Intelligence for Sales Success*, Colleen shows you how to discover your own EI challenges. I think we all have room for growth in this area. (While I'd love to say I've mastered all the EI skills, the truth is, I'm still working on a couple things.) Plus, you'll find tons of strategies in here that you can use right away to strengthen your own EI.

One last thing. Increasing EI has significant financial payback for individuals and teams. Sales revenues go up. Turnover is reduced. Customers buy more and refer more. But don't take my word on it. Get reading!

JILL KONRATH
Author, *SNAP Selling* and *Selling to Big Companies*

Introduction

THOUSANDS OF BOOKS have been published teaching salespeople how to improve their selling skills. For me, there was only one reason to write yet another: to make a difference in the professional lives of others. I strongly believe that the concepts outlined in this book, if applied, are game changers.

I've seen too many salespeople work too hard for the lackluster results they achieve, never attaining the income and satisfaction they desire and deserve. Why? Because they misdiagnose their sales challenges and, as a result, prescribe the wrong solutions. They focus only on improving their "hard" sales skills when, in fact, something far different than just poor selling techniques are getting in their way.

This epiphany came after observing hundreds of role-playing scenarios during sales training in which salespeople flawlessly executed hard sales skills. They set up the meeting agenda properly, asked effective questions, and clearly established the next steps required to ultimately make a sale. But sometimes, when these same salespeople ended up in front of an "Attila the Hun" prospect, every bit of that knowledge and skills training went out the door. The salesperson moved into a "product dump," offering solutions too quickly, even though he or she knew that such behavior leads to a price-driven sale rather than a value-added, consultative sales conversation. Or the opposite behavior occurred: the salesperson simply shut down, unable to think of anything to say, hoping and praying the meeting would end quickly.

What creates this chasm between knowing what to do and actually doing it? The answers are in this book.

There is a Buddhist proverb that states, "When the student is ready, the teacher appears." And luckily for me, the team from Complete Intelligence, LLC, Marty Lassen and Scott Halford, showed up as my teachers and helped me discover the answer to this nagging question. Lassen and Halford are experts in emotional intelligence and work with executives and managers, showing them how to incorporate emotional intelligence skills into their personal and professional roles.

Emotional intelligence skills are rarely taught to salespeople. Most training is focused on hard sales skills such as finding new opportunities, negotiation, or closing tactics. There is little attention placed on soft skills such as empathy, rapport, and self-confidence. Even less on teaching salespeople how to manage their emotions and the emotions of others in order to achieve the sales results they desire.

Some salespeople are good at posing questions to prospects. But if they lack the emotional intelligence skill of empathy, they don't communicate the all-important message, "I really feel your pain and I do care." Despite the good questions they ask, prospects don't connect with them. They feel as if they are being interrogated rather than meeting with a trusted advisor where a true partnership is being forged.

Other salespeople are good at building rapport but have diffi-culty building their sales pipelines. They don't prospect consistently because they have not developed the emotional intelligence skill of delayed gratification. Rather than take the time to strategize and develop a pursuit plan, they give in to the pull of instant gratifica-tion and focus on what is easy instead of what is effective. Proactive business development is put off with the excuse, "I'll do the sales activity when I have time." Their wonderful rapport skills are wasted because they have few, if any, appointments on the calendar.

Still others excel at prospecting, but once they are sitting in a meeting, facing a sophisticated C-level buyer, they lack the emo-tional intelligence skill of self-confidence to close the business at full margin. Under pressure, they quickly cave into negotiation tactics. Emotions take control of the sales meeting rather than tapping into their selling skills, logic, and intellect.

All of these scenarios demonstrate how mastering a variety of emotional intelligence skills can make a huge impact on a person's sales results. After many meetings with Lassen and Halford, coupled with my years of sales and sales management experience, I became convinced that lack of emotional intelligence skills training is a key reason that sales professionals often don't close the gap between knowing and doing. Most sales professionals know what to do. So why aren't they doing it?

Like many of you, I've enjoyed a great deal of success in sales. However, I have also fallen short when it comes to mastering my own emotional intelligence skills. Sometimes my high independence prevented me from asking other people for their help, input, or perspective. I missed out on the wisdom of others that could have provided shortcuts to my goal or prevented mistakes. At other times, my lack of impulse control caused me to make decisions too quickly and say "yes" to things I shouldn't have. Digging out of those "impulse decision holes" has created stress and heartburn for me over the years. I didn't understand the power of the emotional intelligence skill of self-awareness, so I never set aside downtime to accurately assess why the same sales or leadership problems kept appearing in my life.

Perhaps you have experienced the same issues. After reading this book and putting its principles into action, you will quickly discover that soft skills do produce hard sales results.

My Career in Sales

My first exposure to sales was through Jazzercise, a dance fitness company based out of Carlsbad, California. I owned three franchises and quickly learned how to sell and market in order to fill the gymnasium with paying students. I did everything imaginable to bring in business, from hiring my neighbor's kids to stuff flyers in mailboxes to creating a speakers bureau. (Never mind that it was a bureau comprised of one speaker—me!) I delivered talks on fitness and nutrition to anyone who would listen, with the goal of converting audience members into paying clients.

My efforts paid off and my success in building the business landed me a place on the national training team for Jazzercise. I went around the country teaching new instructors how to start and grow their businesses. This was my first exposure to teaching and is where I learned that I had a love and talent for it.

From there, I had the good fortune to join Varsity Spirit Corporation, a small firm based in Memphis, Tennessee, that both manufactures cheerleading uniforms and conducts hundreds of cheerleading and dance camps and events across the country. The timing was right, as Varsity was just starting to build a direct sales force. This company gave many people incredible opportunities for growth, and fortunately for me, I was one of the recipients.

I started in the field as a sales rep and moved up the corporate ladder to become Vice President of Sales, directing a national team of 130. During my ten years at Varsity, we grew from $8M to $90M, went public, and were named by *Forbes* magazine as one of the 200 fastest growing companies in the United States. Varsity is still growing and very successful, now the largest company in the industry.

After this great opportunity, I pursued teaching and training sales and sales management professionals full time, and have been doing that for the last fourteen years. We get hired to "grow" three things: sales, profits, and happiness. Although my firm works with a variety of clients and industries, our customers all have three values in common:

1. They value education and outside advice.
2. They value and invest in their greatest asset, their employees.
3. They treat their vendors like partners.

I am very fortunate to work with great customers.

What You Will Learn in This Book

The topic of emotional intelligence may seem a bit esoteric, but nothing could be farther from the truth. You will find that this book is filled with pragmatic information that you can use immediately. Don't let the "soft" in "soft skills" fool you. The results you will glean from applying this knowledge are anything but soft.

This book will teach you about emotional intelligence in the sales arena step by step. Many of the skills, definitions, and context are derived from the assessment tool, the Emotional Quotient Inventory 2.0 or EQ-i 2.0®, distributed by Multi-Health Systems, one of the world's leading assessment companies. This instrument measures *a cross-section of interrelated emotional and social competencies, skills, and facilitators that determine how effectively we understand and express ourselves, understand others and relate with them, and cope with daily demands.* We use this assessment with many of our clients to establish a baseline of competencies and identify areas of improvement. We know that what gets inspected and measured does improve.

In Chapter 1, we will look at emotional intelligence and its relationship to closing the knowing-and-doing gap. According to the American Society of Training and development, American companies spend about $20 billion (yes, *billion*) a year on sales training. With that many dollars being invested, you would expect every salesperson and organization to be hitting their revenue goals. Yet, sales continue to be a problem for many organizations because they are not addressing the core issue for lack of results, which can be attributed to poor emotion management.

Chapter 2 establishes the foundation of knowledge about the neuroscience of sales to help you understand the unique combination of biology, psychology, and selling skills that go into a successful sales transaction. Salespeople who learn to harness this combination are the ones who will succeed in an increasingly competitive business environment.

In subsequent chapters, each stage in the sales process is examined in order to point out specific soft skills that can improve your performance. For example, a soft skill such as assertiveness makes a big difference in how you set and manage expectations for a partnership, not a "vendor-ship." This knowledge will help you stay out of those frustrating selling scenarios where prospects aren't returning your phone calls or emails. These skills will help you qualify opportunities better—and reduce long sales cycles as well.

You will also learn how impulse control and reality testing help you listen more than you speak. Prospects have been complaining about salespeople talking too much for years and I will give you new tools and insights that will help you talk less and sell more.

And you will discover how the emotional intelligence skills of self-regard and self-awareness affect what level of decision makers you will contact and meet with in an organization. Do you really need one more lecture on "calling at the top"? I don't think so. You know what to do and these soft skills will help you execute.

The book closes with a discussion around the qualities of emotionally intelligent sales leaders and cultures. They have a competitive advantage in the market because they attract and keep top performers. The formula is pretty simple: good people like hanging around other good people. Emotionally intelligent salespeople value relationships, play well with others, are lifelong learners, and show up with good attitudes every day.

Throughout this book, each chapter ends with several "action steps" that provide you with concrete ways to implement the skills you have learned in that chapter and that you will use in your day-to-day sales life.

How to Get the Most Out of This Book

At this point, you might be wondering if I value traditional sales training. The answer is a resounding yes! My company teaches hard sales skills every day. However, I've found that sales performance issues are usually the result of a deficit in both hard and soft skills. It's not an either/or proposition. It's similar to losing weight. If you want the fastest results, diet *and* exercise is the quickest route to success. I want to encourage salespeople and organizations to take a holistic approach when diagnosing sales problems and solutions.

As you read this book, take time to review your wins and losses from the current and previous years. Look at the data from a different perspective. What hard *and* soft skills allowed you to win or lose business during this time?

As you will learn, scheduling downtime helps you gain clarity on how best to change or improve. Hard-charging salespeople often make the mistake of plowing forward without taking enough time for introspection. As a result, they keep making the same sales mistakes in their approach and process. In the words of Steve Prentice, author of *Cool Down: Getting Further by Going Slow* (Wiley, 2007), "You need to slow down to speed up." Take time to step back and evaluate your areas of weakness.

Part of slowing down means taking time to jot down notes as you read this book. Review the notes daily and weekly so that the new ideas and concepts become part of your daily habits and thoughts. Aristotle was right when he said, "We are what we repeatedly do. Excellence, then, is not an act, but a habit."

Finally, be willing to practice your new skills. When you study any of the "greats" in life, whether they are musicians, speakers, or athletes, you will find a similarity in how they achieved their greatness: hours and hours of practice. The good news is that practice is within your full control. You can practice in good or bad economic times. You don't have to get approval or sign-off from your manager to do it. And it doesn't cost you anything but time.

After reading this book, you will join other progressive sales professionals who have elevated their game by learning emotional intelligence skills. I've said it before, but it bears repeating: soft skills do produce hard sales results. *Are you ready for a game changer?*

PART I

The What, Why, and How of Emotional Intelligence and Sales Results

CHAPTER 1

Closing the Knowing- and-Doing Gap

When You Know Better, You Do Better

THE PROFESSION OF SALES has changed dramatically in the last few years. The Internet has made product knowledge a commodity, and the old sales approach of feature-advantage-benefit selling doesn't work with today's savvy, well-educated prospects.

Today's prospects research their potential purchase or vendor, gather the information they need, and start self-diagnosing problems before showing up to a sales meeting with you. Today's prospects don't need more details on features and functions because that information is available on the Internet. They ask salespeople more questions, better questions, and harder questions.

In some cases, the selling opportunity turns into a product knowledge contest between the prospect and the salesperson, with each person focused on showing the other person how smart he is, rather than working collaboratively toward a solution. If you show up armed with only pretty brochures, a list of open-ended questions, and a canned PowerPoint, it will become a quick race to selling on price rather than selling value, or it is the start of free consulting.

Innovation used to be a key competitive edge. But that advantage is shrinking as technology allows competitors to quickly uncover best practices and incorporate them into their businesses. Differentiators disappear and many salespeople look and sound alike. In order to win business, they resort to discounting, which is a quick race to zero and establishes a vendor relationship, not a partner relationship.

So what's a salesperson to do? How do you win business in this new buying environment?

Understanding Emotional Intelligence

Top sales professionals recognize today's changing business environment and are equipping themselves with emotional intelligence skills. The use of emotional intelligence is relatively new in the sales training world, so when salespeople hear the term, they often ask:

- ► What is emotional intelligence? (Should I know or care?)
- ► How does emotional intelligence affect sales results? (Remember, I'm paid for performance.)

What Is Emotional Intelligence?

In simple terms, *emotional intelligence* (EI) is the ability to recognize your emotions, and to correctly identify the emotion you're feeling and know why you're feeling it. It's the skill of understanding what trigger or event is causing the emotion and the impact of that emotion on yourself and others; and then adjusting your emotional response to the trigger or event in order to achieve the best outcomes.

Emotionally intelligent salespeople are strong in both self-management and people management. When a well-informed buyer starts showing off his know-how by firing questions and product knowledge, the emotionally intelligent salesperson doesn't react to the interrogation and turn into a high-paid answering machine. Instead, she's able to manage her emotions and apply interpersonal and critical thinking skills that move the sales interrogation to a sales dialogue rather than a monologue.

EI has been incorporated into leadership and executive training for over a decade. The Center for Creative Leadership, located in Greensboro, North Carolina, has a long history of researching great leaders. When they conducted a study of 302 leaders and senior managers using the Reuven Bar-On Emotional Quotient Inventory (EQ-i), an instrument developed to assess emotional intelligence, their research showed that the most successful leaders score high in self-control, remain grounded when things get tough, and have the ability to take action and be decisive. They are also great communicators. Successful leaders are empathic and listen carefully to understand what a person is saying and feeling.

Top sales professionals know these same qualities that The Center for Creative Leadership found in successful leaders are also important for success in sales. Global Private Banking and Trust salespeople handle the accounts of wealthy clients whose investments go beyond national boundaries.

Their sales team must effectively execute selling skills and also be able to handle the complexities of Canadian and international tax law. This team completed the EQ-i assessment and the results showed that top sales performers scored high in empathy, stress tolerance, and flexibility, similar to top leaders. Leaders buy from leaders, so it makes sense that top performers integrate emotional intelligence skills into their sales process.

In order to understand the power of emotional intelligence, there are two areas to learn about that are rarely covered in sales training programs: the neuroscience of the brain (which we'll discuss in Chapter 2) and the management of emotions, or psychology.

You may think you need to go to graduate school to understand emotional intelligence, but we can translate it into layman's terms by going back to high school biology. In that class you studied anatomy (which deals with the structure and organization of living things) and physiology (the study of the mechanical, physical, and biochemical functions) of the human body (and you thought you were just learning about lungs, kidneys, and the digestive tract!). So take this basic knowledge and apply it to the great Olympic swimmer Michael Phelps, who earned eight gold medals at the 2008 Beijing Olympics.

Like many athletes, Phelps is gifted with good anatomy and physiology: big hands, abnormally long torso, and good aerobic uptake. Many people attribute his success solely to his athleticism. However, a fair question is whether he won due to his athletic prowess (anatomy and physiology) or because he was able to manage his emotions during a highly stressful athletic event? Case in point: During the 200-meter butterfly race, his goggles malfunctioned and filled up with water. In fact, he couldn't see the wall when he touched it with his final stroke. It's reasonable to assume that most people would have panicked and lost momentum. But Phelps managed his emotions, swam his race, set a world record, and collected the first of eight gold medals.

Did he win because of his physical prowess or because of his ability to manage emotions? The answer is yes to both. His success is a combination of biology and psychology. Now, let's look at neuroscience and psychology from a non-Olympic point of view.

The anatomy and physiology of the brain together produce what is referred to as *IQ*, a number used to express the *apparent relative intelligence* of a person. It is the ability to concentrate, organize material, and assimilate and interpret facts. IQ is important in life and business. It's often the reason you get a degree and your first job.

A growing body of research indicates that *EQ*, the ability to manage your emotions, is equally important or more important. EQ is an array of noncognitive abilities. It's the ability to understand what others need, to handle stress, and to basically be the person that others like to hang around with. IQ will get you in the corporate door; EQ will take you up the corporate ladder. Let's face it, a good sales competitor in your industry is going to have a decent IQ, just as a good Olympic competitor is going to possess decent athletic ability. The differentiator is EQ. (How many of you have met the smartest guy in the room and didn't like him, and as a result you didn't do business with him?)

Emotional Intelligence and Sales Results

So let's move on to our second question and explain how improving emotional intelligence can affect sales results.

Millions of dollars are invested in sales training every year but it often doesn't produce the desired revenue or changes. Many well-intentioned salespeople and sales organizations study the art and science of sales. You are one of those salespeople because you picked up this book. You listen to audio tapes, attend selling seminars, and read the latest and greatest literature on sales and influence. You're part of a dedicated group of salespeople that have learned the basic hard skills of selling: ask questions to uncover the prospect's pain, meet with all the buying influences, and get a range of budget before presenting solutions.

You know what to do. So why are so many of you running meetings where the prospect forces you to "show up and throw up"? Why are you talking with non–decision makers and writing proposals without uncovering the prospect's budget? This behavior is often referred to as the "knowing-and-doing gap." You know what to do; however, during tough selling situations you often just don't do it. You walk out to your car or hang up the phone and ask yourself, "*What just happened here? Did my long-lost twin sister take over my body during that meeting? Why didn't I say this or that?*"

Many salespeople review a less-than-stellar sales meeting and blame their poor performance on inadequate selling skills when it may not be about sales technique at all. It's similar to the practice of medicine. If a doctor misdiagnoses the patient's problem, the prescribed solution simply won't work. For example, if a patient has seasonal allergies and the doctor keeps prescribing medication and treatment for a sinus infection, the patient isn't going to get better. The doctor is working on the wrong problem.

Diagnosing Sales Performance Challenges

Many salespeople misdiagnose their sales challenges and work on the wrong problem. They attempt to improve their sales results by focusing on selling skills alone. The root cause for poor sales performance is not just about hard skills; it's often linked to the inability to manage your emotions so that you think clearly and react effectively.

Let's be clear. We don't discount the importance of selling skills. We teach and coach them every day in our business. In fact, teaching selling skills is where we discovered the knowing-and-doing gap. We've worked with thousands of salespeople and watched them execute sales role plays flawlessly during a sales training workshop. But then these same participants land in front of a tough prospect and don't execute the skills they've learned. They buckled, babbled, and sounded like a character out of a bad sales movie. They knew what to do, but didn't do it. This puzzling behavior led us to explore emotional intelligence in order to discover the missing link between sales training and sales results, the gap between knowing and doing.

Sales can be a tough profession with lots of no's and setbacks. If a salesperson scores low on self-control and handling stress, there's a good possibility that when adversity hits, it'll be followed by days of inaction, self-doubt, and roller-coaster emotions. Too many salespeople live exhausting and unfulfilling professional lives because of their inability to handle their emotions and the stress of professional sales.

Emotion Management and Sales Results

A common hot button for salespeople is when a prospect begins to question them about the value of their product or service. *"Why are you so high? Your competitor is half your price."* If you don't recognize this hot button, your emotional response can be to quickly concede and offer a discount. (This occurs even after you've been taught negotiation skills and concession strategies.)

The emotionally intelligent salesperson recognizes the potential hot button, manages his emotion, and changes his reaction. The response is calm and smart: *"The reason our services are on the high end of the investment is because many clients, prior to working with us, had purchased on price. As a result, the purchase ended up costing more because they could never get a live body on the phone for problems. This led to missed deadlines, which affected their reputation and repeat business from clients."*

This redirect is a professional way to introduce the company's value proposition and move the conversation from price to value. You executed an effective selling skill because you didn't allow a tough prospect to trigger your emotions.

Let's take Jolene, who's a sales manager's dream, as an example. She has a good attitude, works hard, and consistently hits quota. She's been selling for about five years and really knows her stuff.

Jolene sells a complex service, and her sales position requires a certain level of intelligence to even understand how the service works. IQ isn't a problem; Jolene earned straight A's in her undergraduate and graduate studies.

But when she schedules a first meeting with the chief technology office (CTO) of a large firm, he turns out to be a difficult prospect. He's not very warm, seems hesitant to engage in conversation, and throws rapid-fire questions at Jolene, like *"I'm not sure if I see the value in your service. We might be able to develop this in-house. Why should I consider using your firm?"*

Although Jolene knows the answers based on the extensive product knowledge training she received from the company, she caves under pressure from this not-so-friendly prospect. She freezes and can't think of the right response. (Her only thoughts are how to end this meeting quickly and how much she'd like to put this difficult prospect in a choke hold.) She doesn't recall one single selling technique and her meeting turns into a product-dump meeting that ends with the prospect saying, *"I'll need to think it over."*

Did lack of IQ, product knowledge, or selling skills cause Jolene's poor sales performance, or was it her inability to manage her emotions during a stressful sales meeting? We contend it's the latter. Jolene just experienced the knowing-and-doing gap, the gap between knowing what to do and being able to do it. She knows what she should say and do, but under stress the "shoulds and do's" went right out the door (which is where Jolene wanted to go during the entire sales meeting) and she was unable to respond. Jolene's emotions got the best of her. She got frustrated and a little intimidated, and neither emotion leads to a good sales outcome.

The good news is that emotional intelligence can be changed and improved with focus and commitment. We challenge you to become a better sales doctor and properly diagnose selling challenges by looking at both soft skills (emotional intelligence) and hard skills (sales ability).

The Business Case for "Return on Emotions"

Not convinced about the bottom-line impact of emotional intelligence? Then take a look at what the Consortium for Research on Emotional Intelligence in Organizations says about organizations using emotional intelligence as part of their sales training and recruitment programs:

- ➤ In a 1996 U.S. Air Force study, 1,500 recruiters were tested to discover common EI traits among recruiters who achieved 100 percent of their quota. *By duplicating those EI traits, retention rate increased 92 percent, saving in excess of $2.7 million.*

- ➤ In a pioneering EQ project, American Express put a group of Financial Advisors through a three-day emotional awareness training. *In the following year, the trainees' sales exceeded untrained colleagues by 2 percent, resulting in millions of extra earnings.*

- ➤ At L'Oreal, twenty-eight sales agents selected on the basis of certain emotional competencies sold on average *$91,370 more than salespeople not tested, for a net revenue increase of $2,558,360.*

So what do they know that other organizations don't know? They've figured out that a combination of IQ and EQ is essential for sales and business results. They understand that there's a business case for "return on emotions."

Discover Your Sales Strengths (Warner Business Books, 2003), written by Gallup consultants Benson Smith and Tony Rutigliano, conducted research that shows that customer satisfaction and future recommendations are based on an emotional connection with the salesperson. Customers who like their salesperson are *twelve times* more likely to continue to repurchase.

Daniel Pink, author of *A Whole New Mind* (Riverhead Hardcover, 2005), writes in his book about the need for soft skills in order to conduct and win business in the Conceptual Age—the age of the knowledge worker. His work shows that the new worker will need to possess *both* high-concept and high-touch skills.

High-concept skills are the ability to synthesize data, recognize trends and patterns, and transfer them to a novel invention or solution. This aptitude is really important, because salespeople regularly meet with information-overloaded prospects who don't have the time to figure out what information is important, what information is largely irrelevant, and how to quickly distill the most valuable information into the best outcome.

As Steven Stein and Howard Book state in their book, *The EQ Edge* (Stoddart, 2000), "A competitive economy demands that we be problem solvers, not problem reporters or collectors." Good salespeople demonstrate their value by being good problem solvers and creative thinkers.

High-touch skills have to do with understanding the subtleties of human nature, finding joy in yourself, eliciting it in others, and pursuing purpose and meaning. These attributes certainly don't sound like hard-core selling or business tactics, do they? This set of abilities is absolutely connected to emotional intelligence skills—the understanding of self and others. And the reality is that high-tech skills and other hard skills are increasingly outsourced to emerging world economies.

Soft skills, such as critical thinking, problem solving, and relationship building, are much harder to outsource or duplicate in a software program.

Hired for Hard Skills—Fired for Soft Skills

Many sales managers make a common mistake of hiring new salespeople based primarily on the number of years in sales or industry experience. This isn't necessarily bad. However, there's a lack of focus on integrating soft skills into their selection process.

When we teach sales hiring and selection workshops, we conduct a simple opening exercise with sales managers to raise awareness on the value of soft skills. We ask the participants to tell us about their worst sales hire. The stories run from downright funny to "you've got to be kidding!" One of the best ones we've heard was the potential sales candidate who reached across the table and grabbed an olive off the sales manager's salad. Do you think he was hired?

More than 90 percent of the reasons for a bad hire consistently relate to soft skills. We hear responses like, "*He couldn't get along with other departments*," "*She had a bad attitude*," and "*He couldn't read people very well.*" Notice that none of the responses are linked to the hard skills of selling, such as "*He just couldn't close,*" "*She didn't meet with the right decision makers,*" and "*He wasn't good at selling value.*"

Lack of soft skills is a big part of the problem in sales organizations not achieving sales results.

Case Study

Martin Seligman, Ph.D., author of *Learned Optimism* (Free Press, 1998), details in his book a well-known case study for "return on emotions." In the 1980s he met with John Creedon, who at that time was the head of Metropolitan Life Insurance Company. Creedon was concerned and frustrated about the company's high agent turnover. At the end of the fourth year, 80 percent of the new agents were gone, which created great financial and personal hardship for the company.

Creedon explained to Seligman, "Selling is not easy. It requires persistence, and it's an unusual person who can do it well and stick with it." (Note that persistence is a soft skill, not a hard skill.)

Seligman introduced a new concept of measuring optimism in potential candidates and worked with Met Life to identify top performers with it. He found that agents scoring in the top ten percent sold 88 percent more than the most pessimistic agents scoring in the lowest tenth. Today, Met Life incorporates measuring optimism in their hiring and selection process. The result is increased revenues and decreased turnover. Optimism, a soft skill, produces hard sales results.

I have a personal bias when it comes to the value of soft skills because of my start in sales. I had the good fortune of landing my first sales job with a small firm in Memphis, Tennessee. When I joined the company, it was moving from a catalog-sales model to a direct-sales-force model. The company was small and didn't have a lot of cash to invest in big base salaries so it was willing to take on salespeople with little or no sales experience. (Me.)

The early sales team was paid straight commission, worked long hours, and went head to head with a better-known competitor five times its size. Looking back on this experience, I now realize this company was extremely good at identifying salespeople with emotional intelligence skills.

The company didn't have many marketing or sales support tools, so it was up to the salesperson to figure it out and often create their own materials. Today, I'd give our early sales team high marks in the emotional intelligence skills of problem solving and independent thinking.

Since there wasn't a formal training program, salespeople called each other to ask for advice on products, sales, and customer service. This willingness to share and help members of a group is an emotional intelligence skill called "social responsibility"—the ability to contribute to a group even though you might not personally benefit.

This early group of sales reps also knew that when selling skills needed improvement, it was up to each person to buy the latest sales guru's books and tapes. This self-improvement behavior is the emotional intelligence skill of "self-actualization"—the pursuit of personal and professional improvement. The company's wisdom in hiring for soft skills certainly paid off, as it is now the largest in its industry.

Soft skills *do* produce hard sales and positive business results!

Action Steps for Improving Your Emotional Intelligence

Emotional intelligence and understanding the what, why, and how of emotions is best discovered through self-awareness and self-discovery. A principle of learning and influence is that people believe their own data. It's your responsibility to discover your own reasons for your actions or inactions.

There are three steps you can take that will increase self-awareness quickly if used every day and every week. They are:

1. Schedule downtime.
2. Create technology-free zones.
3. Name the specific emotion.

Step #1: Schedule Downtime

In order to increase self-awareness, make a daily commitment to be free of distractions and to-do lists. *Self-awareness* is the foundational skill for building and improving other emotional intelligence skills. It helps you gain insight into how you're showing up each day and how your attitude, behavior, and actions affect yourself and others. "Know thyself" is a simple definition for self-awareness.

We've seen many a bad selling scenario, like Jolene's, repeated because the individual didn't take the time to reflect and analyze how they got into a sales meeting with less than desirable outcomes. (Was the prospect simply shopping your company to get a necessary third bid? Did the prospect have no buying authority? Do you really need to write more practice proposals?) If you don't invest any time in examining your behavior, you will end up in the same free consulting or price-shopping sales chair again and again. Don't keep making the same mistakes. Reruns might be nice for your favorite movie, but bad sales reruns aren't worth the price of admission. Here's the basic principle: no awareness, no change, same outcome. You cannot change that of which you are not aware.

It's only during downtime that you can be introspective and take time to reflect on your actions or inactions. In *Emotional Intelligence* (Bantam Books, 2005; 1st edition, 1995), author Daniel Goleman writes about Richard Abdoo, former Chairman and CEO of

Wisconsin Energy. "Richard has a firm resolution to reserve eight hours a week for solitary reflection. In Richard's words, '*You have to force yourself to spend some time away from the hustle and bustle of your job in order to get down to reality again.*'"

Downtime allows you to ask yourself thoughtful questions to gain clarity on your sales behavior and outcomes:

- ➤ What was the reason for my reaction to the prospect or customer?
- ➤ What would have been a better response during the sales meeting?
- ➤ What can I do differently to prevent getting into a dead-end selling situation?
- ➤ Who do I need to ask for help and perspective?
- ➤ What did I do well and how do I repeat that behavior?

We worked with a wealth-management client named Joe who had an "ah-ha" moment after learning the self-awareness concept.

Joe is one of those guys who appears to have it all. He's good-looking, funny, and likeable. He cares about his clients, works overtime to ensure that every client need is taken care of, and is ethical in all of his dealings.

So we were a little puzzled to learn that he wasn't achieving his revenue goals. Joe told us he got a little defensive when potential clients questioned his strategies or philosophy. Like many sales-people, Joe misdiagnosed the real issue and tried to solve the problem by applying more selling skills, like validating the prospect's concerns and redirecting the conversation to better understand their question.

The problem was that his nonverbal communication shouted irritation, giving the prospect a not-so-comfortable experience. Joe further analyzed and asked himself thoughtful questions about why he reacted defensively to certain questions from prospects. He realized that he was stuck in the past and still reacting to an overly critical father who, when Joe was growing up, dismissed many of his ideas and thoughts, often calling them "stupid" or just "not very smart." Joe worked hard to prove his father wrong by getting good grades and a good job, but the emotional fallout from the criticism in his youth stayed with him into adulthood. When a prospect asked a question, Joe interpreted the question as an insult to his intelligence. He reacted with defensive posture, behavior, and language.

Once Joe recognized the root cause for his emotion and consequent reaction, he was able to reframe questions from prospects as just questions, not criticism or doubt about his abilities. Joe changed his response and improved his sales results.

Step #2: Create Technology-Free Zones

The very idea of turning off their electronics is enough to send most salespeople into severe withdrawal. However, a real deterrent in achieving downtime is our recent addiction to technology.

Salespeople, like those in other professions, feel a constant need to be connected. Many salespeople today remind me of dogs with shock collars. The minute something buzzes, rings, or vibrates, they feel a need to grab it regardless of time, place, or who they're speaking with. (Have you ever found yourself competing for attention with a smartphone?)

Many salespeople don't allow themselves time to think because they're so busy checking their text messages, email, and voicemail. Contrary to popular opinion, the brain isn't good at multitasking. The frontal lobes of the brain require focus in order for a new habit to begin forming. The only habit many salespeople have is that of one constantly checking their electronics.

A high-level, consultative sales meeting takes a full hour of being totally present and engaged. Due to their constant checking in and frequent interruptions, many salespeople have lost their ability to focus for more than ten minutes. (We even see salespeople checking their smartphones during appointments!) The prospect senses the lack of attention and the sale goes to the focused, attentive salesperson. We call this behavior *SAD*: *sales attention disorder*.

You can cure SAD by developing a new sales habit: introspection and reflection. It's right in line with creating downtime. Create technology-free zones just like no-smoking zones. Wake up fifteen minutes early each morning and simply devote time to thinking about the following:

- How do I want to show up today with my boss, colleagues, and customers?

- Do I want to be the go-to person in the office or the go-away-from one in the office?

- Where did I not show up well yesterday?

- What caused me to respond ineffectively? Effectively?

- Where will I be tempted not to manage my emotions today?

I have a lovely piece of art in my family room, which is where I spend between fifteen to thirty minutes of reflection time each morning. The words on it are always a good reminder of how I want to interface with employees, colleagues, clients, and prospects: *love, joy, peace, goodness, patience,* and *self-control*. If I accomplish even half those words, I'm bound to have a good day!

Step #3: Name the Specific Emotion

When analyzing your own knowing-and-doing gap it's important to be specific about the emotion you're feeling. For example, if you tell your sales manager that you're nervous about calling on the C-suite when in reality you're downright intimidated, you'll both be working on correcting the wrong problem.

There's a big difference in prescribing a solution for being nervous and for being intimidated. Nervous can simply mean you're excited about the opportunity. It can mean that you're prepared rather than complacent.

Intimidation is a different emotion with different outcomes. If you're intimidated, you show up to the C-suite lacking confidence and personal presence. Maybe you feel the person you're meeting with is better than you in some way because of his titles and degrees. After all, your business card reads Business Development Executive, not Vice-President. And you have no academic credentials or certifications listed. (How in the world will this prospect take you seriously?) You're worried that the prospect is going to know more than you do. So you invest all your pre-call time worrying about looking and sounding smart instead of focusing on your prospect's business and challenges.

A key concept we teach to solve the intimidation factor is helping you realize you are being self-centered. Yes, the thought of being seen as self-centered hurts. However, look at your actions and thoughts and you'll find that you may be dialed into the What About Me Channel: *"How do I look and sound?" "Is the prospect impressed with me?"*

Apply the emotional intelligence skill of empathy. Empathy is the ability to understand what others are thinking or feeling. Step into your prospect's shoes and really think about the life of this C-level executive. She has multiple roles and responsibilities, sixty hours of work sitting on her desk, and is constantly being asked to do more with less. Do you really think she has time to focus and study various products, services, and solutions as you do? No, she needs a great salesperson to be a valuable shortcut and make her life easier. She needs you!

Shift your focus and turn on a new channel: It's All About Them. As the late Dale Carnegie said, *"You can make more friends in two months by becoming interested in other people than you can in two years by trying to get other people interested in you."* We think Carnegie had some insights into emotional intelligence.

We'll continue to diagnose and prescribe throughout the book because there's no one magic answer for increasing emotional intelligence and sales results. Get some downtime, put your electronics in their place, and clarify what emotion you're feeling and why you're feeling it. Are you making up stories or working from empirical data? Are you still responding to events from childhood?

Analyze whether your response is serving you well and what you need to do to change. If you don't have the answer, ask your boss, colleague, or coach. Trusted colleagues will help you see your way out of the emotional-response forest.

The emotionally intelligent salesperson knows that outside stimuli cannot always be changed (tough prospects and customers, stress, putting out fires, busy calendars, etc.). But she also knows that her reaction to stimuli can be recognized, controlled, and improved by increasing her self-awareness. Congratulations on taking the first step to increasing your revenues and happiness by integrating emotional intelligence skills into your sales process!

CHAPTER 2

The Art and Neuroscience of Sales

The New Way to Influence

MANY SALESPEOPLE have heard the saying, "Sales is an art and a science." We think it's time to update this phrase for today's business environment to, "Sales is a combination of art, science, and neuroscience."

The art of sales pertains to your ability to size up the prospect, determine their personality style, and adjust your selling style to create rapport and trust. It involves your ability to read and connect with the buyer by paying attention to nonverbal clues, such as a shift in body language or a change in the prospect's tone of voice.

The science of sales involves following a defined sales process and applying specific selling skills at each stage. For example, business development requires executing strong value propositions; uncovering the prospect's story involves specific questioning and listening skills; and, at the solution stage, skills such as storytelling and presentation come into play.

The *Merriam-Webster Dictionary* defines neuroscience as "a branch of the life sciences that deals with anatomy, physiology, biochemistry or molecular biology of nerves and nervous tissues and especially with their relation to behavior and learning." "Behavior" and "learning" are the key words here. Knowledge of neuroscience elevates both the art and science of sales because it ensures that salespeople behave consistently in executing the influence skills they have learned in order to produce sustainable sales results. As discussed in Chapter 1, many salespeople know what to do—and still don't do it.

Sales professionals experiment with a lot of different tools in order to be more successful in sales. They read about the law of attraction: "Think about your goals and they will come."

They write positive affirmations: "I am happy, successful, and wealthy." And each morning, they wake up believing and achieving.

Then a tough sales or account management situation occurs, emotions take over, and the only thing salespeople are attracting and believing is self-doubt and frustration. According to Dr. John Arden, author of *Rewire Your Brain* (Wiley, 2010), "You cannot change how you think and feel without changing your brain." In other words, unless you actually change your mental pathways, new behaviors, responses, and skills will not be executed. And the better you understand how your brain works, the more likely you are to be successful.

Selling to the Old Brain

Start your education about the neuroscience of sales by learning about a part of the brain called the *amygdala*. The amygdala is an almond-shaped cluster of connected structures that lie directly above the brainstem in each hemisphere of the brain. It is the oldest part of the brain, often referred to as the "old" brain or "reptilian" brain. The amygdala is part of the *limbic system*, which is a group of structures associated with emotions and experiences that help detect a threat. It's the emotional alarm system of the brain and screens all stimuli coming into the brain and decides what's safe or not safe. It's similar to the stoplights we use every day. Red is stop, green is go, and yellow is proceed with caution.

This screening of information occurs without conscious thought. The amygdala has the ability to override other parts of the brain, including the cognitive, rational center located in the *prefrontal cortex*, the front of the brain and the part that is involved with planning complex cognitive behaviors. When the old brain senses danger, it automatically produces a fight, flight, or freeze response. Heart rate increases, as does the production of adrenaline to prepare your body to react.

To get a better understanding of this structure, let's look at two examples, one where the amygdala works in your favor and one where it doesn't.

You've probably experienced the positive benefit of the amygdala many times. Take a situation where you are driving down the highway and, unexpectedly, the driver in front of you slams on the brakes. If the prefrontal lobes of the brain were in charge, and not the amygdala, you would tell yourself, "Gee, the dumb driver in front of me is braking unexpectedly. I'd better take my foot off the gas, steer to the right, and put my foot on the brake." By the time this logical conversation ended, you would have been in an accident. Instead, the amygdala took over, sensed danger, and executed the automatic response to brake and adapt—without logical thought or reasoning.

Now, let's go back to prehistoric times and study the caveman. His daily life was primarily focused on food, shelter, and safety. On more than one occasion, he probably encountered an animal, such as a bear. Upon such a meeting, his amygdala signaled danger, eliciting a fight-or-flight response. If the caveman chose to fight, there is a good chance he lost to a bear with sharp teeth and claws. If he chose to flee, the bear was probably faster; either way, the bear probably enjoyed a tasty lunch.

(Just so you know, if you ever encounter a bear, the correct response requires emotion management, or engagement of the prefrontal lobes where logical, rational thinking occurs: stand still [no flight], remain calm [no fight], and talk to the bear in a soothing voice.) Since emotional intelligence training wasn't around in early times, we are pretty sure the caveman defaulted to a flight-or-fight response.

Why Good Salespeople Can Buckle During Difficult Selling Situations

How does the understanding of neuroscience improve sales results? We aren't being chased by bears, though some tough prospects and customers do a nice job of imitating one.

Picture this selling scenario: You are meeting with three prospects for the first time. Two of the prospects are engaged and friendly. They are asking and answering questions, and are fully present. The third prospect is not engaged in the slightest and is happy to let you know it. He is looking at his watch, checking his smartphone, and every bit of his nonverbal communication is telling you that he does not want to be at this meeting.

This aloof and hostile behavior can elicit a fight-or-flight response if you are not trained in emotional intelligence and the basics of neuroscience.

Fight or Flight

Let's take a look at some fight responses shared by clients during some of my sales training workshops. Perhaps you can relate to a few of them. When working with a hostile prospect, the following might happen:

➤ Salesperson gets more aggressive and leans forward toward the prospect.

- ➤ Salesperson talks faster and louder.

- ➤ Salesperson gets defensive and the tone of his voice is sharp and short.

- ➤ Salesperson goes into a product dump to prove how smart she is.

- ➤ Salesperson tries to engage the hostile buyer by asking specific questions.

- ➤ Salesperson delivers sarcastic responses to the question, "Why are you so much higher than your competitor?" *"Well, Mr. Prospect, you get what you pay for,"* or *"Are you looking for a Yugo or a Cadillac?"* (Yeah, that's a response the prospect hasn't heard before.)

Flight responses are equally interesting, and can look and sound like these:

- ➤ Salesperson ignores the hostile prospect, hoping the meeting floor will open up underneath her chair. She turns her focus to the two engaged prospects and ignores Mr. Grumpy.

- ➤ Salesperson discounts too quickly. When the non-engaged buyer finally speaks up and asks, *"Can you do this for 10 percent less?"* the emotionally charged salesperson immediately concedes to a price reduction.

- ➤ Salesperson agrees to write a practice proposal. The non-engaged prospect has responded to questions with only short, one-word answers. We call them "grunt" sales meetings. At the end of the sales meeting, this same prospect asks the salesperson to put together a proposal. The salesperson, in flight mode, answers, *"Yes, I can put together some recommendations,"* even though he doesn't have a clue about the prospect's needs, budget, or decision-making process.

The Knowing-and-Doing Gap

The fight-or-flight response, triggered by the inability to manage emotions, is often the root cause for the lack of sales skills execution. You know you are supposed to follow your sales process, but under pressure you fall into the prospect's buying process. You actually can't recall certain skills or responses that you have been taught.

Here's why: it doesn't have to do with will or skill—it's Biology 101. When you get emotionally charged, the blood moves from the digestive tract to the muscles and limbs in preparation for fleeing or fighting. (The amygdala thinks you are in front of a bear.) Heart rate goes up, adrenaline is released, and clarity of thought is compromised. All your selling skills are lost in a fray of emotion and, in many cases, you are left with the communication skills of a monkey.

Another reason you may not execute the right response is that you have not practiced new skills and behaviors enough for them to land in *long-term memory*. Long-term memory is the ability to recall information. For example, most adults can still sing the *A,B,C* song learned in grade school. Others can recite scenes from a favorite movie. Short-term memory is just what it sounds like. You can only recall information—a phone number, a person's name—for about thirty seconds. (Ever gone to a party, been introduced to someone, and two minutes later you can't remember their name?) Focused rehearsal and repetition is the only way that data transfers from short-term memory to long-term memory.

Due to lack of "sales rehearsal," salespeople revert back to old, ineffective responses because they haven't updated old habits and responses, currently in their long-term memory, with new, more effective responses.

We tell our clients that they must practice a new skill at least 144 times in order for the skill to land in long-term memory. We figured by the time someone has focused and practiced a skill or response this many times, there will be change in their brain structure. It's a number that definitely gets salespeople's attention and makes them realize that they are not putting in the time and effort to achieve mastery.

John Wooden, one of the most successful coaches of all time, won ten NCAA championships in a twelve-year span while coaching at UCLA. Wooden coached his players on basketball skills *and* emotion-management skills. In his book, *Wooden on Leadership* (McGraw-Hill, 2005), he said he stressed to his team that "losing your temper will get us outplayed because you'll make unnecessary errors; your judgment will be impaired." "Manage your emotions or they will manage you," he warns. His advice is as applicable to sales professionals and sales teams as it is for basketball players.

The Emotionally Intelligent Response

There is a third response to a difficult prospect other than fight or flight—the emotionally intelligent response. The successful salesperson is aware of negative triggers and chooses not to respond or react to them. She manages her emotions and addresses the "sales elephant" in the room. (The "elephant in the room" refers to an obvious truth that is being ignored or unaddressed.) The sales elephant is big and visible. In Mr. Grumpy's story above, it's obvious to all that the hostile prospect doesn't want to be at this meeting. People of influence don't dance around the elephant; they dance with it.

Instead of ignoring the obvious, the emotionally intelligent salesperson calmly stops the meeting and states the truth: *"I really appreciate all of you taking the time to meet with me today. But Tom, I'm getting the feeling that we should be taking the meeting in another direction. Am I correct?"*

The question isn't delivered with anger or nervousness. It's stated calmly because it is simply referring to what everyone in the room is already highly aware of. We call it "truth telling," and it is a powerful influence skill. From Coach Wooden's perspective, this is managing your emotions as opposed to letting your emotions manage you.

Calling out the elephant in the room, or truth telling, requires a knowledge of neuroscience as well as emotional intelligence skills.

First, you must be aware of the natural physiological response to perceived danger. Awareness is always the first step to any permanent change or improvement. Then, because of your heightened awareness, you can identify the trigger and make a conscious choice to remain calm and cool by applying two emotional intelligence skills.

1. Self-awareness—the ability to know what you are feeling and why; it's the ability to choose how you want to appear to others.

2. Assertiveness—the ability to state nicely what you need: "I can't write a proposal if you aren't talking to me."

Case Study

A client in the marketing and branding business shared the following story after learning more about neuroscience and emotional intelligence.

Sue was a presenter at a regional conference. One participant, Bob, was very impressed with her and enthusiastically asked to set up a meeting with himself and his partner. Two weeks later, Sue was meeting with Bob and his partner Rich. Bob started the meeting by sharing all the good ideas he heard from Sue at the conference. He also asked several questions about Sue's services and clients.

Sue and Bob were having a great time. However, Rich made it very clear that he didn't want to be at the meeting. He didn't ask any questions, his body language was defensive, and he kept checking his smartphone.

It didn't take a psychic to read this situation. It was a selling situation where a salesperson could have chosen to end the meeting quickly (flight), confront Rich (fight), or nicely state the truth. Because of her training, Sue chose the third option and stopped the meeting.

"Bob, I really appreciate you inviting me in today. It's always nice to know someone likes your work. However, Rich, I have a feeling that what Bob brought me in to talk about today is really not high on your priority list."

Rich immediately shot back, "It's not."

Instead of responding to his somewhat rude behavior, Sue redirected again and said, "That's what I thought. What do you suggest we talk about?"

Rich did have a different agenda item, as it related to marketing and branding. The sales conversation went another direction—the right direction for the circumstances—and two months later, Sue had a new client.

Here's the question: Did Sue win that new piece of business on selling skills or emotional intelligence skills? We contend it's a combination of both. But we do know that mindset wins over selling skills every time. If Sue had not managed her emotions and addressed the sales elephant in the room, she would not have had the opportunity to use her consultative and problem-solving skills. Soft skills do yield hard sales results.

Walk a Mile in Your Prospect's Shoes

It's important to remember that your prospects also have an amygdala. Many salespeople have been taught ineffective selling skills that don't take brain structure into account.

For example, salespeople have been taught the ABC rule: Always Be Closing. Put yourself in the poor prospect's shoes (and brain) and think of the pressure she feels during a sales meeting when the salesperson is doing a bunch of obvious trial closes. *"So Ms. Prospect, if we can solve that problem, would you want to move forward?"* (It's painful to even type this statement.) The amygdala senses danger because the salesperson asked a leading question. The prospect is worried that any information shared will be held and used against her in a court of sales. As a result, the prospect shuts down, and what started as a consultative conversation moves to a superficial conversation with no real sharing of problems or goals.

Emotional intelligence is about common sense, and leading questions don't make any sense. What is the prospect supposed to say? *"No, I have really learned to enjoy this problem. It's fun to see money wasted at the company."*

Prevent Fight-or-Flight Responses from Your Prospects

We teach our clients to employ a safer approach to keep prospects feeling safe because we don't want to sound the alarm in the amygdala. When prospects feel safe, they share more information, which in turn helps the salesperson put together the right recommendations. Here are a couple of examples:

➤ **Typical approach:** *"Are you having issues with technology?"* Questions that start with "are you" can be interpreted by the old brain as setup questions for the big close. The prospect thinks, *"If I answer 'yes, I'm having issues,' this salesperson is going to start selling me."* So the prospect becomes guarded and so does the sales conversation.

➤ **Safe approach:** *"I'm not sure if you're having issues with technology. But if you are, let's you and I figure out if these challenges are big enough to invest time and money in solving. I know you have a lot of priorities competing for your attention."* This approach is nonthreatening. It puts the prospect in control of the meeting and reverses the roles of each person in the meeting. You also show empathy by stating that you know how many directions your prospect is being pulled. It's now up to the prospect to convince the salesperson that the problems are high on the priority list to get resolved. When people feel they have control, they feel safe and engage more openly in conversation.

Are You Insane?

You may have heard the old saying, "Insanity is repeating the same behavior and expecting different results." Sales can be a tough profession. It's even tougher if you keep repeating the same selling mistakes. Sadly, many salespeople choose to be average rather than strive to be excellent. The puzzling part about this is that mastery of emotions and skills is in a salesperson's full control because you can actually change the way you think, process, and react to events. A bad economy and good competitors don't prevent you from becoming masterful.

Repetition is the key to mastery, and understanding the neuroscience behind this statement should inspire you to incorporate practice into your daily sales life.

Here's the simplified version. You are born with about 100 million neurons. Each neuron has the ability to make up to 15,000 connections, called "synapses." One repetition can create a neural pathway. The formation of neural pathways is called "neuroplasticity." "Cells that fire together wire together" is a common phrase used to describe this action. It's similar to weightlifting. The more you exercise a muscle, the stronger it gets.

The exciting news about this information is that you have the ability to learn new skills and form new habits of thought and response. There was a time when people thought that once something was hard-wired in your brain, you were stuck with it. Recent discoveries in neuroscience are proving that the brain has an incredible ability to adapt and form new neural pathways. The brain's plasticity is what enables us to keep learning.

You *Can* Teach an Old Sales Dog New Tricks

This is of particular importance for salespeople. Old selling techniques don't work with today's buyers, and sales pros need to learn new skills. With repetition and focus, old sales dogs can learn new tricks by creating new neural pathways.

There is a catch, though. In order for new neural pathways to form, you must be focused and willing to practice. Learning is a function of your frontal lobes, and it requires attention in order to promote neuroplasticity and move things from your short-term memory and, eventually, to your long-term memory.

Focus is a problem in sales and business. Many uneducated companies allow salespeople to use laptops and smartphones during presentations, sales meetings, and sales training. Instead of actively listening and absorbing content, these salespeople are busy answering emails and instant messaging. Sales managers shrug their shoulders and say, "The world is changing. We just have to accept this new generation."

The problem is that, no matter how much technology has

changed, the way you learn, remember, and master new information has not—and won't, because of the way the brain is structured. If you're distracted during sales training or sales meetings, information will not be retained. Individuals and companies waste a lot of time and money because they don't know how to harness the power of the brain for sales results.

Stop buying into all the new excuses for not paying attention. If you're serious about becoming masterful at sales and influence, get serious about focus.

The Sales Athlete

Athletics are a great place to study the concept of neuroplasticity. Coaches and their team members have figured out how to improve performance better than the business world. (Ever seen a football player texting on the practice field?)

The coach introduces a new play to the team playbook. Now, does the coach have the team run the play once and expect masterful execution? No, athletes practice more than they play. They run drill after drill in order to create new neural pathways that allow them to execute the play without even thinking. Under stressful game situations, athletes don't fall back on their old habits, because the process of neuroplasticity has replaced and upgraded those habits.

During one of the basketball games played at the 2011 NCAA tournament, the crowd watched with mouths open as a player took his time, dribbling the ball with only fifteen seconds on the clock. His team was behind by one point and he needed to make the shot. Ten seconds, five seconds, and then swoosh—the ball was through the hoop! It was a beautiful example of managing emotions and the execution of a skill accomplished by hours of practice on the court.

Let's look at an example from the sales world. Value propositions are part of every salesperson's playbook. Done well, they are powerful tools for opening up new opportunities and sales conversations. Learning a customized value proposition is not hard. It can be as brief as three sentences that state the problems your product or service solves for a client.

However, when we go into sales organizations and ask the sales team to state their value proposition, we often hear stammering, stuttering, or, better yet, "Let me start over."

Not too impressive. (If you learned the Pledge of Allegiance in second grade, we are pretty sure that with focus and repetition, you can learn three sentences.) So what's the reason so many salespeople are lacking this skill? It's lack of commitment, lack of focus, and lack of repetition. They have not developed the value proposition neural pathway.

There is no shortcut to success. You must practice in order for the neurons to fire together, wire together, and create a new neural pathway. If you are not willing to practice, then you must be willing to accept average sales results.

Putting It All Together

Let's bring all of the concepts in this chapter together. A trusted referral partner has introduced you to a prospect. The prospect has been very busy, so you were not able to have a very good up-front qualifying conversation. But the referral partner told you, "This is a done deal."

The meeting starts and you ask the prospect what he would like to put on the agenda. The prospect replies, "Tell me a little bit about your company. We are not sure if we need to outsource this or do it in-house." (So much for this deal being done and won.)

Not yet trained in emotion management, you go into panic-and-pitch mode. You turn a simple statement from the prospect into an objection and start trying to overcome it. *"Well, Mr. Prospect, here are some of the reasons you should consider outsourcing this project to us instead of doing it in-house."* There is no probing, discovery, or building of rapport. There are a lot of attempts at closing, which results in setting off an alarm in the prospect's amygdala. Danger, danger: salesperson in the room trying to force a close.

If you have been trained to manage your emotions, you will agree with the prospect and refrain from overreacting. You heard the prospect make a statement, not an objection. You know that the only way you can help the prospect determine the best course of action is to ask questions. *"Well, Mr. Prospect. You may not need to outsource this. Let's have a discussion on the pros and cons of both options. At the end of this meeting, I think we'll be able to figure out whether you need to outsource or can do this work internally."*

Same selling scenario, same event, with very different outcomes. The first meeting involves a vendor focused on closing, which usually results in chase mode or buying on price. The second meeting is collaborative and based on a partnership mindset. If a sale is made, it will be on value, not price.

Action Steps for Improving Your Ability to Influence

So how do we get out of the cycle of fight or flight? What can you do to take your skills, attitudes, and behavior to the next level? The good news is that there's plenty that can be done, and it's in your control. There are three steps you can take:

1. Make a decision to change, grow, and improve.
2. Identify triggers and change the response.
3. Practice, practice, practice.

This first recommendation may surprise you, as it doesn't refer to emotional intelligence or neuroscience. However, if you don't take this first step, don't bother with any of the others.

Step #1: Make a Decision to Change, Grow, and Improve

We have a favorite phrase around our office: "The only time you can afford *not* to change, grow, or improve is when your competitor has made the same decision." During a sales meeting for US Foods, Spencer Warren, the company's vice president of sales for Colorado, used a funny analogy in asking his team to make a decision about doing more cold-calling.

He explained that he grew up on a 3,000-acre ranch. Part of ranching is climbing on and over fences. "You know," he said, "you have to make a decision to put your feet on one side of the fence or the other. Straddling is just not a comfortable place to be."

Many salespeople are professional straddlers. They say they want to get better, but their calendar doesn't show any indication of that. There is no time marked off for personal improvement or practice. The lure of reality TV seems to win more often than the lure of mastery. Many salespeople talk about success, but aren't willing to take the steps to walk down that road.

During a coaching session with one of our clients, things got a little tense because the client was straddling the fence. She had not learned her value proposition, couldn't ask ten basic questions, and wasn't doing the necessary activity to fill the pipeline. Her excuse was, "I don't have any time." My response was, "Do you drive to work? What's your commute time and what are you doing with that time?"

Drive time can be a perfect time to practice skills or listen to a CD that reinforces skills and concepts. Time wasn't the problem. The problem was that this client had not made a decision to become great. Have you?

Malcolm Gladwell, author of *Outliers* (Little, Brown and Company, 2008), created quite a stir with his book by sharing research on how to become an overnight success. It was fairly straightforward: 10,000 hours or 10 years. He noted that talent is a factor in success. However, studies show that talent combined with commitment to immerse oneself in their area of expertise is the winning formula for "overnight success."

In his book *This Is Your Brain on Music* (Penguin Group, 2006), neurologist Daniel Levitin tells us that, in study after study—whether of composers, basketball players, fiction writers, ice skaters, concert pianists, chess players, or even master criminals—10,000 hours is the number that comes up again and again to achieve the mastery that is associated with world-class experts.

You might be a little discouraged reading this because you are 9,500 hours away from mastery. But please remember that improvements will happen on your journey to mastery. Make a decision. Do you choose to be average or masterful?

Step #2: Identify Triggers and Change the Response

Awareness is the first step to any type of change. Top salespeople debrief every sales meeting, good or bad, to identify what they did right and where they could improve.

Armed with the knowledge of emotional intelligence and neuroscience, top salespeople also identify what triggers from the prospect may have thrown them off their game. They are highly aware that they can't control the triggers. However, they can control their response.

Here are a few scenarios we have heard from salespeople where triggers from prospects have created an emotional response.

> ► "I find myself getting annoyed when a prospect keeps me waiting. I start making up stories like: this prospect doesn't respect my time; this meeting is going to be a waste of time. By the time the meeting starts, I know I show up a little defensive."

> ► "I know I overreact when the prospect starts asking about price right away during the meeting. Instead of applying

good selling skills that redirect the conversation, I find myself getting tongue-tied."

▶ "My big trigger is when the prospect is checking their email during our meeting. I know that I should ask them to either turn it off or reschedule. Somehow, the words get stuck in my mind and never come out of my mouth."

Here is a great tool to change your response: *change your story!* When salespeople examine the why behind the reaction, they find they are creating the nonproductive emotions from the stories they are telling themselves. Salespeople are great fiction writers. They talk to themselves, make up stories, and pretty soon they have turned their fiction novel into a best-selling nonfiction book. Here are some examples:

▶ *The Buyer Who Keeps You Waiting:* Change the story to, "Wow, this person must be really busy. This is a good sign because he is probably the type that is looking for a partner or a shortcut because he doesn't have time to analyze and solve his problems."

▶ *The Buyer Who Talks Price Early:* Change the story to, "I can't blame her for asking about the price. Most prospects aren't sure what questions to ask, so they ask the one they know: 'What's this going to cost?' This will be a fun meeting as we explore other things she should be considering."

▶ *The Buyer Who Is on Email.* Change the story to, "My fault. I forgot to set the expectation that we will need a one-hour, uninterrupted meeting. I will nicely ask him to turn it off or, if he is in the middle of a firefight, to reschedule."

Change your story and you will change the emotional response.

Step #3: Practice, Practice, Practice

When you see someone who is masterful, you can be assured there are hours of perfect practice behind their mastery. A great keynote speaker has often practiced a one-hour speech 100 times before delivering to a live audience.

There are two ways to practice: physically saying and doing the skill, or visualizing yourself executing the skill.

Physical practice requires making a decision and setting aside time on your calendar to meet with a colleague or coach. It means asking someone to role-play with you to practice different areas of the sales process. If you are making a cold call, practice. Call your voicemail and listen to your tone of voice and inflection. Would you buy from you?

If you're preparing for an important sales meeting, practice setting up expectations for time, meeting agenda, and outcomes. Create customized value propositions for the buyer based on position and industry, and practice saying them over and over. If you know you answer questions too quickly during a sales meeting, practice redirecting and clarifying skills.

Mental practice—visualizing—is another example of the incredible power of the brain. Research shows that when a person is visualizing an activity, the same part of the brain lights up as if the person is actually engaged in the activity. Athletes have long incorporated this practice into their training regime.

A powerful example of visualizing comes from Major James Nesbeth, who was a POW in North Vietnam. During his seven years of imprisonment, he was in a small cage where he couldn't even stand. Nesbeth used the power of visualization to keep his sanity and his mind sharp.

Each day, he would play a game of golf. He was very specific, visualizing all aspects of his game and replaying every detail in his head. When Nesbeth was finally released, he found that he had cut twenty strokes off his golfing average without having touched a club in seven years.

This is the power of the brain. Nesbeth formed new neural pathways that led to success in golf without even walking the course.

Now, let's qualify this story for sales. As a sales professional, you will need to leave your office and play the course.

Visualization is part of pre-call planning. Create a picture of you running a highly successful sales meeting. Experience the emotions of this successful meeting. You are calm, in control, caring, and competent.

Picture the prospect being engaged, respectful, and interested. See yourself asking good questions, smart questions, in order to arrive at the best recommendation. When you do this repeatedly, you create new neural pathways for thoughts, behaviors, and skills.

It's time to step up your sales game. Apply neuroscience and emotional intelligence to your business development and sales process. The knowledge will help you achieve and believe. Emotional intelligence is the new competitive edge for sales professionals.

PART II

Emotional Intelligence and the Sales Process

CHAPTER 3

Prospecting

The Real Reason for Empty Sales Pipelines

THERE ARE BASIC CAUSE-AND-EFFECT SITUATIONS in life. If you don't water your plants, they wither and die. If you don't exercise, there is a good chance you will gain weight. And if you don't fill the tank with gas, expect your car to stall on the highway.

There are similar cause-and-effect situations in sales. If you don't prospect consistently and effectively, you will experience empty sales pipelines, cyclical sales cycles, and inconsistent results.

Every salesperson knows that consistent prospecting is essential for achieving revenue goals. Business development activities vary by industry, life cycle of the company, and sophistication of the company's marketing department. However, many salespeople are still responsible for generating some or all of their own opportunities.

So why do so many salespeople struggle with sporadic, ineffective prospecting efforts? Why do companies need a CRM tool to make sure members of their sales staff are doing what they signed up to do: prospect, acquire, and retain customers?

Salespeople and sales managers throw various training solutions at this prospecting problem. Goal-setting workshops are held to set specific sales activity metrics. Time management skills are taught for better organization. More sales training is delivered on value propositions, referrals, and social media. Strategy is discussed to determine who is a good prospect and how to approach them. All of the above are good efforts that too often result in short spurts of sales activity and motivation, soon replaced by salespeople sitting at their desks surfing the Internet in non–work-related activity.

Success in prospecting requires a combination of hard selling skills, emotional intelligence skills, and awareness of how to sell to the "old brain." Soft skills such as delayed gratification, interpersonal skills, reality testing, and stress tolerance are often overlooked when diagnosing inconsistent or ineffective prospecting. Most value propositions, a basic sales skill used in prospecting, are not designed to sell to the old brain. The result is prospecting conversations that never convert to an appointment.

Let's take a closer look at the soft skills, hard skills, and the neuroscience behind effective prospecting.

Are You a Sales Marshmallow Grabber?

In 1972, Dr. Walter Mischel, a Stanford University psychology researcher, conducted a study that's often referred to as the "marshmallow" study. He gathered a group of four-year-old children together and placed a marshmallow in front of each one. Mischel told the children he would return in about twenty minutes and if they didn't eat their marshmallow, they would receive another one.

Now, you're four years old with a delicious marshmallow sitting in front of you. What would you do? Some children quickly grabbed the marshmallow, while others waited patiently for Mischel's return. Mischel continued his research, following the children for fourteen years. The results are pretty amazing. The kids who waited and did not grab the marshmallows scored 210 points higher on SATs, were more socially competent, and experienced more personal and professional success than their marshmallow-grabbing peers. These children demonstrated an emotional intelligence skill called "delayed gratification." They were willing to wait before achieving the reward. The marshmallow grabbers demonstrated instant gratification: "I want it and I want it now."

So what does marshmallow grabbing have to do with prospecting and sales success? Salespeople scoring low in delayed gratification get frustrated easily. If one hour of prospecting by phone, email, or social media doesn't yield results, they give up. If they don't meet a prospect at an association meeting, they quit attending meetings. When their instant-gratification need is not met, business development stops or slows down.

Research from the National Sales Executive Association shows that most salespeople quit pursuing an opportunity after four prospecting attempts. This same research shows that most business is closed after five to twelve outreaches. In many cases, you have skilled salespeople not hitting revenue goals simply because they give up too soon on their prospecting efforts.

Another problem created by the need for instant gratification is lack of planning and analysis and a consequent lack of development of a strategic pursuit strategy. Salespeople scoring high in delayed gratification will devote the necessary time to analyze their business in order to receive the reward of investing *future* prospecting time in the right places with the right prospects. Salespeople not putting in the time to plan are often busy—but not productive. These are the salespeople who are making cold calls, sending prospecting emails, going to networking events, involved in associations, and proactively using the social media tools. Their calendar is full; their sales pipeline is not.

Busy or Productive?

Salespeople, like other professions, get caught up in the daily rat race for success. Many are running a full-blown campaign to be president of the Busy Club. (How many of you have ever compared calendars with a colleague, bragging about how busy you are?) "Busy" doesn't always mean "effective."

The excitement of being busy often clouds the true results of your prospecting efforts. Salespeople scoring high in delayed gratification take time each month and quarter to determine what sales activities are producing the best results. Then they do the logical thing: invest more time in those activities.

It might be time to hold a truth-telling session with yourself and ask the following questions about your prospecting activities:

- ▶ Is social media working for you or are you just avoiding talking to real prospects?

- ▶ How many connections have you made on LinkedIn that resulted in contacts and client acquisition?

- ▶ Are you attending networking events that yield a good time but no clients?

- ▶ Are your referral partners referring or just meeting you for lunch?

- ▶ How many referrals are you asking for and receiving?

- ▶ Are your articles generating leads or writer's cramp?

- ▶ Do you have lots of friends on Facebook and no clients?

- ▶ Do you know your conversion rate from activity to appointment to close?

Case Study

A client of ours, KPA, helps businesses comply with regulatory compliance and loss control. This is a disciplined sales team that has defined metrics and measurements in place. Upon analysis, its members found that cold calls were not producing results. This wasn't due to a lack of sales skills, as this team had crafted very good value propositions. Through further analysis, they discovered that their best source of leads was referrals from existing clients. As a result, team members increased their focus on strategies and tactics to add even more value to existing client relationships to keep referrals coming. The result is that all members of this sales team are achieving their quota in a tough business environment.

Apply the emotional intelligence skill of delayed gratification. Slow down and analyze your business development activities. Figure out whether you are being productive—or are just busy.

Fish Where the Fish Are

Salespeople who thrive on instant gratification also waste time running appointments with prospects who are never going to buy. It's a simple formula. If you want to catch more fish, then fish where the fish are. Salespeople who are addicted to instant gratification fish in the wrong ponds. You can have the best pole, bait, and gear, but if your fishing hole is only full of minnows, you will not catch a trout.

When conducting a win-loss analysis with clients, the first question we ask is, "Should you have been at the appointment in the first place?" No amount of hard selling skills will help you win business if you are showing up to meetings with prospects who don't fit your ideal client profile.

Analysis of your business requires that you be skilled in delayed gratification because you need to take time to evaluate your best clients, determine what makes them good clients, and then apply that information to identifying future sales opportunities.

Can you describe your best-fit clients? These are clients you enjoy working with and wish you had twenty more just like them. There are two areas to examine when identifying your best-fit clients: demographics and psychographics.

Demographics includes criteria such as revenue, number of employees, locations, SIC code, and stage of growth. What is often missed in the analysis is an equally important criterion called *psychographics*, which classifies clients by their attitudes and values.

When we help salespeople analyze their sales activity plan, we start by asking them to describe their favorite client. Here are the attributes we hear 90 percent of the time:

- ➤ They value relationships, expertise, and shortcuts.
- ➤ They value outside counsel and outsourcing.
- ➤ They treat their suppliers like partners, not vendors.
- ➤ They treat their employees well.
- ➤ They are involved in philanthropic causes.
- ➤ They are proactive in seeking solutions.
- ➤ They value relationships.
- ➤ They genuinely value expertise.
- ➤ They are committed to win-win relationships.

Note that all of the items listed above are psychographics, not demographics. It's important to include both in your analysis of where to fish.

Like our clients, we are charged with prospecting and closing business. Otherwise, we have no one to train and coach. We have found two key psychographics that raise our close ratios. The first is that our potential client believes in hiring outside advice. They are not "do-it-yourself-ers." The second psychographic they possess is that they view education and training as an investment, not an expense. When we have those two criteria in place, our close ratios go up by as much as 30 percent because we are fishing in the right pond.

We work with an investment banking firm, Capital Value Advisors. When we conducted this exercise with them, they shared one of their key qualification criteria: the NJR rule. Translation: No Jerk Rule. CVA knows they win more business and get better results when they work with nice people (not jerks) who treat them like partners and value their expertise. This might be criteria you want to consider adding to your qualification list.

Review your business and analyze your "fish." Determine where you and your company play best and win business. Analysis takes time and does not feed the instant-gratification monster. Think of those four-year-olds and don't be a sales marshmallow grabber.

Plan Your Work and Work Your Plan

Salespeople start out with the good intention of prospecting each week. The problem is, their calendars don't reflect this intention. When we work with sales teams and ask them to tell us the times they have scheduled in their calendars for prospecting, the usual response is, "Uh, I haven't taken the time to calendar-block my schedule." In other words, there is no plan for proactive prospecting. Pretty soon a month goes by, very few hours of focused prospecting occurs, and the sales pipeline experiences yet another drought.

Before you invest in one more timesaving gadget or time management training seminar, examine the biggest timesaver at your disposal: your ability to delay the gratification of doing something fun and exciting instead of planning and organizing. One more gadget or course in time management is not going to help if you don't develop your delayed-gratification skills. You must put in the work of planning before you will get the reward of a day or a week that runs efficiently.

Planning your work week means you have to slow down and think. As Henry Ford said, "Thinking is the hardest work there is, which is probably the reason so few people engage in it." It's recognizing that you will not get the same adrenaline rush with planning as you do when helping a client with a customer service issue or running an appointment. Planning requires delayed-gratification skills because the reward for a full sales pipeline and consistent sales results are in the future, not that day or week.

Once you have made the commitment to plan, block out specific times for proactive prospecting and honor those times as if they were gold, because they are!

Emotion Management and Planning

Successful salespeople score high in managing their emotions. They don't overreact to positive or negative selling situations because they are aware of triggers that cause such responses and make a conscious choice on how they want to show up each day. Emotion management is important in your prospecting efforts and here's why.

Pete attends a time management workshop and learns to set specific times for prospecting on his calendar. His new discipline is rewarded and he connects with a prospect by phone. They have a good conversation and Pete suggests that he and the prospect meet. The prospect says she is free next week, exactly during the hour Pete has set aside for prospecting. Pete gets excited (doesn't manage his emotions), gives up his committed hour, and sets the appointment. He is now headed down the path of sporadic prospecting and cyclical sales results.

Top salespeople manage their emotions and their calendars. In this situation, they simply reply, "Ms. Prospect, unfortunately I am booked at that time. I am open at 2:00 P.M. that day—would that time work for you?"

Use your delayed-gratification skills and emotion management to plan your work and work your plan.

Drive-By Relationships

In a high-tech world, instant gratification is everywhere. We have same-day delivery, instant messaging, and drive-through restaurants. Things are getting less personal and people are trained to expect and get quick results. The problem in the sales profession is that you are dealing with human beings, not things. We remind our clients that processes are efficient, but relationship building is not.

Salespeople are taught to build networks and relationships with referral partners. Both are powerful strategies for finding new prospects and filling the sales pipeline. Research shows that a salesperson referred into an opportunity increases her close ratio by as much as 50 percent over a cold lead.

The bad news is that this strategy is not well executed by most salespeople due to their inability to build relationships.

Salespeople possessing high interpersonal skills value people and take time to build and retain relationships. They have the ability to give and take in order to create meaningful social interactions because relationships are built over time, not in a first meeting. (Do you really think someone is going to introduce you to their best client if they don't know you or trust you?) The strategy of building referral partners and relationships applies whether you are meeting with a potential partner in person or online in the new Sales 2.0 world.

Salespeople with high interpersonal skills are connected and are connectors. These good relationship builders ask themselves two questions every day:

1. Who is the best/right person for me to connect with today to help me grow my business?
2. What can I do today to help a colleague or client grow their business?

When a company meets with us to discuss referral or networking training, the first question we are asked is, "Can you teach my sales team how to get more referrals?" There are definitely hard selling skills needed for success; however, sales training alone generates fewer results if there is not an equal emphasis on soft skills training.

The first skill we teach in referral partner training is the "give goal." This is a powerful tool for building and keeping relationships. The give goal means you set a weekly sales activity metric for giving and helping clients, colleagues, or referral partners. Generosity is a key trait found in salespeople with high interpersonal skills because they genuinely care about their clients and partners.

Giving can be introducing your client to a potential prospect. It can be sending an article of interest that will help clients or partners in their business. It can be inviting them to an event to meet other prospects or partners. Host a joint webinar and send an invitation to both of your customer databases. Set a meeting to go over your client list to see what introductions are of value.

We have a give goal of five at our office, where we strive to make a deposit in our clients' and referral partners' "relationship account" five times each week. We know it works because our sales pipeline is full.

The give goal is also based on research from Dr. Robert B. Cialdini's book, *Influence: The Psychology of Persuasion* (Harper-Business, rev. ed., 2006). Dr. Cialdini discusses six principles of influence in his book, one being reciprocity. His research shows that when you give a person something, he feels obligated to reciprocate. Salespeople who practice the give goal reap the reward of partners and clients wanting to reciprocate.

Case in point: When you receive free, personalized address

labels from a nonprofit organization, do you feel obligated to write a check in order to keep the labels? I do. That's the principle of reciprocity at work.

Here are just a few questions to ask yourself to see if you are acting as a connector, a giver, and a relationship builder:

▶ Do you know your referral partners'/clients' value proposition? (*If you don't, how can you give good introductions?*)

▶ Do you know your referral partners'/clients' goals for the current year? (*If you don't, how can you identify opportunities?*)

▶ Have you set a goal for giving referrals? (*Are you a giver or a taker?*)

▶ How many lunches have you set up to introduce your referral partner(s) to other partners, clients, or prospects? (*Or are you too busy to connect?*)

▶ How many calls of introduction have you made on behalf of your partners or clients? (*Or do you subscribe to the lazy way of networking by saying, "Call Joe and use my name."*)

Case Study

One of our clients shares a good story about building a solid referral partner relationship.

Ryan Coy is a rep for Source Office Products, an office supply company. Commercial real estate brokers are a good potential referral partner for him because they both call on the same prospects and clients. Brokers often are very guarded with their client list because they get hit up by a lot of speed networkers trying to tap into their contacts with business owners. We define *speed network-ers* as salespeople who have one cup of coffee with a potential referral partner, check off "relationship building" on their daily to-do list, and then are confused by lack of referrals coming in the door from their new best friend.

Ryan made it a point to use both delayed gratification and interpersonal skills to build a relationship with this broker. During the course of the year, they met for lunch several times and got to know each other personally and professionally. Ryan made intro-ductions that generated business for the broker. Nine months into the relationship, his interpersonal skills paid off. The broker felt he could trust Ryan and is now reciprocating with introductions that have resulted in thousands of dollars of closed business for him.

Develop and improve your interpersonal skills. You will improve relationships, receive more referrals, and enjoy repeat business.

Sales Reality Check

Let's flip to the other side of the sales equation and talk about the hard-working salesperson who does all the right stuff. This is the salesperson who calendar-blocks, prospects consistently, and is a good partner for her clients and colleagues. Her sales pipeline is full but revenue goals are not being achieved. The underlying problem for her lack of sales results is a combination of soft and hard sales skills.

Here's the scenario. Jill is a disciplined salesperson. Her consis-tent prospecting pays off and she connects with a prospect. During the conversation, the prospect shares his pain, telling Jill, "*We are getting really lousy customer service. We think it might be a good time to look at other vendors.*" Jill lets her emotions get the best of her and gets excited. She "buys the buying signal." As a result, she gets sloppy in her qualification process, and quickly sets an appointment before the prospect changes his mind.

Jill puts the prospect into the sales pipeline and shows up to the appointment. After an hour of conversation, the prospect decides it's only fair to give the existing vendor one more chance. After all, they have been doing business with this vendor for ten years. Jill just wasted her time with a suspect, not a prospect. What went wrong?

Hope Versus Reality

In order for Jill to achieve better sales results she needs to improve her qualifying skills by developing the emotional intelligence skill of reality testing. Simply put, this is the ability to see things objectively instead of as what you hope or wish they would be.

We discuss this skill a lot with clients because it's easy for salespeople to get excited when a prospect shares a challenge or shows interest. It's important to remember that an interested prospect is just that—interested, not qualified.

Salespeople scoring high in reality testing ask both tough and real-world questions. They know hope is not an effective selling skill. If a prospect has been working with another vendor for ten years, he must be able to convince you during the qualifying conversation that there is enough pain to switch relationships.

For example, "*Mr. Prospect, I can understand your frustration with ABC company. However, you've been doing business with them for ten years and relationships are important. Is this problem really big enough for you to take a look at switching vendors or do you just need to have another conversation with ABC company?*"

Now it may shock you that the salesperson has given the prospect an out, a reason to say no. What is he thinking? This rep values his time and is testing the reality of the situation. He is conducting a sales conversation that is a real-world and honest one. (Do you like switching vendors for phones, insurance, or financial planning?

I don't.) Switching vendors can be a hassle, and many of us put off making a change. Your prospects aren't any different. It's the salesperson's responsibility to manage emotions and test the reality to determine if this prospect is just whining or really ready to make a change.

Top salespeople don't live in the land of hope and denial. They test the reality of a potential opportunity to make sure they are running an appointment with prospects, not suspects.

Are You Stressed Out?

Every salesperson has experienced a drought in their prospecting activity. You know, it's when every prospect you talk to says, "I'm happy with my existing supplier," "We have no money," or "I am new on the job—can you call me in six months?" Repeated dead ends can be stressful and negative self-talk sets in. "No one is buying, I must be losing my touch" or "I wish I had a better product to sell." (It's always nice to blame the company.)

Stress is caused by our perception of an event rather than the event itself. When the economy tanked in 2008, salespeople who scored high in stress tolerance said, "Good, this tough economy will get rid of some of our less qualified competitors." Their perception of the event was positive, not negative.

Prolonged stress produces *cortisol*, a stress hormone that over time results in fatigue and lack of creativity. The stressed-out salesperson doesn't have the energy to prospect or the ability to see new ways of bringing in business. Sales activity falls off, as do sales results.

"Don't Worry, Be Happy"

Salespeople scoring high in the emotional intelligence skill of stress tolerance have the ability to withstand adverse events without developing physical or emotional symptoms. They bounce back quickly after setbacks and disappointments. These salespeople generally score high in optimism, firmly believing that tomorrow or next week will yield better results.

When working with these top performers, we find they look at life through a different filter, one that allows them to be positive about future sales results, even in difficult times. As Benjamin Franklin once said, "While we may not be able to control all that happens to us, we can control what happens inside us." Franklin sounds like he was an emotionally intelligent man.

Here are three thought processes we have noted in salespeople who manage stress and, as a result, consistently achieve sales results.

1. **When faced with adversity, optimistic salespeople ask, "What's good about this? Where's the lesson that is going to serve me well when I go after the next big opportunity?"** Top salespeople know that adversity builds character. Adversity is also where the greatest lessons for future success are learned. These salespeople know that when the going gets tough, most salespeople go—to try and find greener pastures. *Top salespeople don't look for greener pastures; they* make *greener pastures.*

2. **Optimistic salespeople choose their friends wisely.** Jim Rohn, the late entrepreneur, author, and motivational speaker, once said, "You are the average of the five people you spend the most time with." This quote isn't just motivational rhetoric. Psychologists know that emotions can spread. The clinical term is "emotional contagion" or "transmission of moods." Research has shown that people will start acting and responding like the people they spend time with. Look around. Are you hanging around with naysayers or yes-doers? Are you hanging around excuse makers or revenue producers? Mom was right. Tell me who your friends are and we will tell you what you are like.

3. **Top salespeople use humor to relieve stress and stressful situations.** When I started in the sales training business, I made a minimum of twenty-five cold calls a day. At times, it could get tedious with no answers or flat-out noes. I learned to inject humor by starting the call with, *"Hi, it's Colleen Stanley. This is a cold call. You may want to hang up."* The response was always a laugh and permission to deliver my value proposition. I always asked for a referral even after I got a no. During one cold call, the prospect asked, *"Why in the world would I refer you? I don't even know you."* I replied, *"I know you don't, but if you did, you would love me."* The prospect and I had a good laugh. He still didn't give me a referral; however, the humorous exchange went a long way toward alleviating the stress often associated with cold-calling.

Prospecting is part of your sales job and it doesn't have to be stressful. Change your perception toward prospecting and you'll change your outcomes.

The Neuroscience of Prospecting

Most sales training doesn't even address selling to the old brain when trying to improve prospecting results. As a result, many hardworking salespeople get discouraged because their prospecting efforts are not paying off.

A key selling tool used in prospecting is the delivery of a value proposition. Whether you are networking, email prospecting, cold calling, or writing marketing copy, the value proposition is the sales conversation starter.

One of the biggest mistakes in selling to the old brain starts with how value propositions are created. The typical value proposition is very logical and focused on the seller's benefits, not the buyer's challenges: "We have been in business fifty years, have good customer service, and a deep bench of expertise." Besides being very boring, this approach lacks emotion. People buy emotionally, not logically, and the old brain is the emotional center of the brain.

Good value propositions need to create "word pictures" in order to influence and persuade the old brain because the old brain doesn't connect emotionally with intangible information. It needs tangible input. The old brain also likes information that is visual. Neuroscientists have shown that the old brain receives images much quicker than other stimuli, which is why value propositions need to paint word pictures of the problems you can solve for potential clients.

For example, a value proposition that states, "We can improve efficiency and output by decreasing downtime in your production lines," is using intangible language and doesn't really paint a picture of the problem the prospect is experiencing.

Tangible language creates a picture where the prospect can visualize the problem you can solve for him: "We work with companies that are frustrated with production lines jamming and, as a result, have a lot people standing around getting paid to do nothing." Do you *see* the difference in the two statements? Which one stirred an emotional response in you?

Selling to the old brain means you must use the same language your prospects use in their daily life. The old brain likes familiarity, and intangible language is not familiar. A value proposition must sound the way your prospect thinks and speaks. We call it "layman's language." How many of you go home and say you had a productive, efficient, and streamlined day? No, you probably go home and say, "I got a lot of stuff done today." Use everyday language when crafting value propositions to better connect with prospects and the old brain.

Let's look at the difference between intangible and tangible, everyday value propositions:

INTANGIBLE: We have superior customer service.

TANGIBLE: We work with clients who are tired of wasting time stuck in voicemail trees and never talk to a live human being. (*Can you see a picture of a person on hold?*)

INTANGIBLE: We help companies win more business.

TANGIBLE: We work with companies who are tired of losing to price after spending hours working on a proposal. (*Can you see a picture of a salesperson sitting at his office, late at night, writing a proposal?*)

INTANGIBLE: We have a one-stop solution for our customers.

TANGIBLE: We work with companies that are tired of managing multiple vendors and piles of invoices. The accounting department wastes a lot of time trying to figure out who to call when a service issue comes up. (*Can you see a picture of a person looking at a stack of invoices or making a bunch of phone calls?*)

There's a reason for the expression, "Pictures paint a thousand words." Get good at painting word pictures when developing your value propositions. When your words help the old brain see the problem you can help solve, your prospect is more likely to engage in a sales conversation.

Action Steps for Improving Your Prospecting Results

Consistent and effective prospecting is key in order for you to hit desired revenue goals. It is a common best practice that we see in top sales professionals. They don't wait for their sales managers to "get on them" to do the work because they know that business development is their responsibility, their job. Here are a few tips for improving this important selling stage.

1. Make a decision.
2. Ask yourself the tough questions.
3. Plan for success.
4. Manage your emotions.
5. Get an accountability partner or a coach.

Step #1: Make a Decision

This statement will be a recurring theme throughout the book. Make a decision on whether or not you want to be in sales and are willing to do the work required of the entire job, not just the parts you like. We've discussed reality testing in this chapter, so here's a reality check. All professionals have parts of their job they don't like. Can you imagine a doctor saying she doesn't like dealing with insurance companies so she is just going to treat patients and ignore the paperwork? Or an accountant saying he doesn't like the hours that go with tax season, so he goes home early during this busy time of year? You'd say that's ridiculous behavior because that's what these professionals are paid to do. Top salespeople are paid to prospect so it's equally ridiculous behavior if they don't do it.

Step #2: Ask Yourself the Tough Questions

Are you a marshmallow grabber looking for instant returns without putting in the daily and weekly sales activity necessary for results? Are you taking time to develop relationships with potential partners or trying to shortcut that whole relationship thing? What's your attitude and self-talk like when adversity hits? Do you sound like a winner or a whiner? Asking tough questions requires emotional self-awareness in order to answer the questions honestly. Get some downtime and figure out if and where you need to change your attitudes and behaviors.

Next, ask yourself questions to determine your why and what.

1. Why do you want to make more money?
2. What are you willing to do to reach your income potential?

Examining your why and what involves the emotional intelligence skills of reality testing and emotional self-awareness. Where is the objective data that shows you are willing to do the work of prospecting, skill training, and relationship building? Have you taken any time to think about your why and what?

Take this reality test to see if you are doing what it takes to elevate your selling skills and results:

- Do you read or listen to an average of two business/sales books a month? (*Or do you go home and watch reality TV?*)
- Do you seek advice from mentors, boss, and colleagues? (*Or do you use the excuse that "successful people are too busy to meet with me"?*)
- Do you practice selling and influence skills two hours a week? (*Or do you keep running very average sales meetings that end in "we'll think it over" or "your price is too high"?*)
- Do you write down your yearly, quarterly, monthly, weekly, daily goals with specific action steps and deadlines? (*Or do you say what average salespeople say: "They're in my head"?*)
- Do you attend a minimum of two educational workshops each year that help you grow personally and professionally? (*Or do you wait for someone else to invest in you?*)
- Have you increased your sales activity to compensate for longer buy cycles? (*Or are you waiting for the good old days to return?*)

A sales training colleague, Dave Tear, shares this statement with his clients who are not executing their business development plan: "I'm listening to what you're saying and I'm watching what you're doing. What I'm hearing is not matching what I'm seeing." Dave teaches his clients reality testing by pointing out that their actions and words don't align.

Step #3: Plan for Success

Use your delayed-gratification skills and put together a business development plan. A critical component of this plan is to establish key performance metrics for each activity. Numbers don't lie and, without them, you can't tell if you are running ahead or behind your plan. It's the number one way to test your reality and keep you from relying on hope as a strategy.

Few salespeople and sales teams have a quantifiable plan. When we ask potential clients about their prospecting plan, we hear vague answers such as, "We do some LinkedIn, some networking, some trade shows, and some cold calling." "Some" is not a number, so we don't know if they are doing one sales activity or ten sales activities a month.

For example, a specific business development plan could be:

- ► 125 outreaches a week—cold calls, warm calls, email prospecting.

- ► One marketing touch with your top ten prospects. Send a link to an article of interest, invite him or her to a webinar, send an e-book, or make a phone call of introduction.

- ► Attend six networking events a month.

- ► Meet with two potential referral partners a month to discuss mutual business opportunities.

- ► Contact a client with something of relevance other than trying to sell them something.

- ► Write two blogs a week.

- ► Work on LinkedIn connections two hours a week.

- ► Write one article a month.

► Set a give goal—help a colleague or client five times a week with something that helps them grow their business.

Top salespeople usually have five or six different ways to generate opportunities each month. They know that one month, this particular business development activity will yield results, and the next month, a different activity will yield results. It's like a good financial portfolio because the prospecting plan is diversified.

Here's another reality check. Consistent prospecting is in your full control. A bad economy, strife overseas, or arguments between political parties in government does not prevent you from making calls and connections.

Step #4: Manage Your Emotions

More than once we have heard a salesperson say, "I just didn't feel like prospecting today. I wasn't in the mood." (Let's hope your biggest competitor doesn't feel like prospecting that day either.)

Top salespeople don't always feel like prospecting. The difference is that they prospect regardless of how they feel because they don't allow emotions to run their life.

Good salespeople manage their emotions by managing their self-talk. Self-talk is what you say to yourself, and the conversation can be positive or negative. There is endless research that shows what you think and say to yourself impacts your actions. Negative self-talk, as it relates to prospecting, sounds like, "No one is buying in this economy, I'm going to get stuck with a tough gatekeeper, they already have an existing vendor, my decision makers are really tough buyers, and no one is going to answer the phone or my email." And guess what, you are right. Because whatever you say to yourself long enough becomes the truth. It's called a self-fulfilling prophecy.

Positive self-talk sounds like:

► "Successful salespeople do what unsuccessful salespeople won't do. Plan, prospect, and prospect some more."

- ► "The race is not to the swift but to those who keep on running."
- ► "Do the upfront work so you can do the fun work."
- ► "I am willing to put in the work to earn the reward."
- ► "Prospects are open to hearing what I have to say because I can make them money and make their life easier."
- ► "Everyone I talk to is friendly and open to a conversation."
- ► "I always find prospects that are ready to buy and invest money."

You get to choose the conversation, and top salespeople choose the positive.

Step #5: Get an Accountability Partner or a Coach

There is a reason Weight Watchers is one of the most successful weight-loss programs in the country. They have weekly check-ins on progress of weight loss to hold everyone accountable. Find someone with whom you can engage in a no-excuses call on sales activity and results every week.

When I started in the sales training business, I had a colleague who was one year ahead of me in the business. He sent me his activity plan and results from his first year. The plan was pinned on my office wall where I could see it every day. When I didn't feel like doing the activity, I reminded myself that if Bob could do it, I could do it.

So what are you waiting for? There are prospects who need your services. Today is the day to let them know how you and your company can be of service. As an early mentor once told me, "The only time you can fail in prospecting is if you fail to prospect."

CHAPTER 4

Likeability

All Things Being Equal, People Buy from People They Like

COMMUNICATION EXPERTS preach the importance of building trust with people in order to build relationships. Sales managers, salespeople, and sales trainers all endorse the importance of trust in winning and retaining business. But here are the hard facts. No prospect is going to trust you after one conversation—and they shouldn't. You haven't demonstrated the execution, follow-through, or results needed to really earn trust and loyalty. No client is going to keep doing business with you if they don't like you (unless you are lucky enough to be the only game in town).

The reality is that likeability is only the first step toward building trust, winning business, and retaining clients. But it's a really, really big one!

The power of likeability and its importance in the sales profession really hit home to us when we were running a meeting with a large general contractor. Its executive team was very frustrated, having just lost a $100 million project to a competitor it considered far less qualified for the job. When we asked why they lost the business, we were surprised to hear the answer: "chemistry." We were expecting to hear answers like "price," "our portfolio wasn't deep enough in that vertical," or "expertise on the project management team." You can imagine the company's disappointment over losing a sizable project to something as soft and fuzzy as "chemistry." We're not referring to the Thomas Edison type of chemistry here, of course, but to that of being liked by a prospect and connecting with all members involved in a selection process. Simply put, business was lost because the contractor's competition was more likeable.

A similar story, with a happier ending, comes from another client who runs a marketing firm. She landed a nice-sized contract. Knowing her new customer had interviewed several competitors, she asked why they selected her company. The answer: "It just felt better around here." Hmmmm . . . was the new client talking about the comfort of her office chairs? No, she was referring to chemistry and the soft skill of likeability.

So what makes one salesperson more likeable than another? Can you actually teach someone to be more likeable? And come on, if you clearly have a better product or service, wouldn't the prospect make their buying decision on that criteria rather than a popularity contest?

Research consistently shows that people scoring high in likeability are hired, promoted, and win business more often than peers scoring low in this area. Many organizations don't win their fair share of business because they forget to incorporate likeability into their overall business strategy.

Companies invest thousands of dollars in marketing and operations. Their website is updated, marketing collateral is professional, and they tweet relevant information daily. Their operations are efficient, using just-in-time delivery, state-of-the-art equipment, or in-the-cloud solutions.

But organizations neglect to put systems or training in place to make their people more likeable. A well-known sales mantra is: all things being equal, people buy from people they like.

All things not being quite equal, people still may buy from people they like.

Here's a scenario we've seen too many times. A salesperson follows up on a lead and goes to the appointment armed with marketing material and confident in his company's ability to deliver the best solution. He has the best products and services; however, due to his inability to read the prospect and connect with a variety of buyers, he loses to a more likeable competitor.

The salesperson didn't know how to adapt his communication style to match the prospect's. His approach seemed a little canned and he ignored the change of energy in the room after a tough question was asked—to which he delivered an okay answer, but not the right answer.

Chances are, your education has been focused on reading information, not reading people. Have you ever taken a course to improve your likeability quotient? Have you ever been taught how to pay attention and tune into what another person is thinking or feeling? What's needed to win business in many instances are emotional intelligence skills such as self-regard, empathy, building and maintaining good interpersonal relationships, and self-actualization. These skills are what help sales professionals become more likeable, and in highly competitive selling situations, they can be the deciding factor in who wins the business. Soft skills will help you stop losing sales to that crazy thing called "chemistry," and are what will be discussed in this chapter.

Would You Buy from You?

The first step to becoming more likeable is to ask yourself a basic question: Do you like yourself? Don't panic; this chapter isn't going to be a therapy session. However, it's important to recognize a basic principle in life: you can't give away something you don't have. If you are not confident and comfortable with yourself—possessing the quality of self-regard—it will be hard to make others feel confident and comfortable with you.

The first step to increasing your likeability is to accept yourself, your strengths *and* your weaknesses. Salespeople who score high in the emotional intelligence skill of self-regard like themselves, warts and all, and are confident in themselves and their abilities. They don't have a problem acknowledging when they make a mistake or admitting they don't have all the answers. This balance of confidence and humility makes them authentic, real, and, well, just plain likeable.

Confidence, Authenticity, and Likeability

We experienced the power of confidence combined with authenticity while attending a sales training conference a few years ago. One of the speakers was a successful vice president of sales, running a large sales organization. It would have been very easy for this gentleman to get onstage and boast of his success, as many of his less-confident peers did throughout the conference.

Instead, he began his presentation by sharing a story of how he blew a recent sales call. The story included him getting lost on the way to the appointment, arriving late, and forgetting business cards, as well as spilling a glass of water on one of the key decision makers because he was harried and hurried. His perfect storm of mishaps had us holding our sides with laughter. This speaker's high self-regard allowed him to admit and share his not-so-perfect sales meeting. His humility and humor ingratiated him to the audience because he was confident, authentic, and likeable.

Authenticity is touted as one of the key qualities needed to influence and persuade people. And yet it seems difficult for many salespeople to apply it in their daily sales role. In our years of observing hundreds of role plays and actual sales calls, we have seen genuine, authentic people turn into insincere salespeople. Their slick alter ego shows up during a sales meeting and they engage in impression management, trying to show the prospect how smart they are. Product knowledge is spewed or there is a slow death by PowerPoint, touting the greatness of the salesperson's company. Or they turn into sales robots, using every sales technique known to man. *"Bob, thanks for sharing. So Bob, I think you will agree that we have the best solution for your needs."* Who talks that way in everyday life?

Here's the basic formula. If the prospect doesn't think you're authentic, she also won't believe your product or service offering is authentic. No prospect is going to invest time or money in fake products, services, or people.

"How do you or can you teach someone to be more authentic? More likeable?" We posed this question to Michael Allosso, a communication expert and leadership coach. Michael shared the top two things he sees in authentic people: confidence and preparation. "Confidence comes from knowing that you are prepared. And when you are prepared, you can relax and be yourself."

Hearing his comment made perfect sense, because in our work with top sales performers, they do the up-front work. They apply their delayed gratification skills and take time to do pre-call preparation, which allows them to show up more confident and relaxed at a meeting. They write out the questions they want to ask during the meeting. They prepare appropriate responses to the potential objections or questions the prospect will ask. They have checked out the website, LinkedIn profile, press releases, and corporate reports. Value propositions are memorized and conversation is easy because they put in the time to achieve the "10,000 hours" mastery goal.

Top performers are prepared, and when you are prepared, it's easier to take your authentic self to the sales meeting.

Case Study

Carol is a successful salesperson. She has high self-regard, enjoys her work, and doesn't take herself too seriously. During a sales training workshop, she shared the following story with the participants.

Carol met with a prospect and got stumped answering a few questions. She admitted to the group that she ran an ineffective meeting because she didn't do the necessary pre-call preparation. (Note that she did not blame anyone but herself for her actions.)

Carol returned to her office and called the prospect to acknowledge and apologize for a lousy meeting. She used humor and blamed her poor selling skills and preparation on her evil twin sister. The prospect was impressed by her authenticity and accountability in owning up to an ineffective sales meeting. He invited her back for a second meeting—and she ended up closing the business.

There are two emotional intelligence skills working here. First, Carol's emotional self-awareness allowed her to diagnose the root cause for a poor sales meeting: lack of preparation due to arrogance because of her previous success in closing business. Second, her self-regard allowed her to accept her poor performance, move on, and ask for forgiveness and a second opportunity. Carol's confidence, authenticity, and humility make her likeable.

It's All About *Them*: The Prospect and Customer

Top salespeople scoring high in likeability also score high in the emotional intelligence skill of empathy. Empathy is the ability to be aware of, understand, and appreciate the feelings and thoughts of others. It is the ability to see the world from another person's perspective. We often refer to it as the ability to "walk a mile in another person's shoes without ever actually putting them on." In top salespeople, empathy shows up during meetings because of their ability to listen, build rapport, and as a result, be liked by prospects and clients.

The problem we see in sales is that many people leave this important skill at home or in the car when they step into their role of a sales professional.

Here's a classic scenario we've observed many times. The prospect shares a problem such as, "I am really frustrated with deadlines being missed by my current vendor." The salesperson, focused only on his own needs, barely acknowledges the prospect's pain and answers, "Great! Is there anything else we should cover?" (The prospect doesn't think this problem is great.)

Or, the salesperson immediately starts giving solutions without really gaining full perspective on the problem and its implications. Neither response is empathetic and doesn't do much to increase likeability during a meeting.

The empathetic salesperson puts herself in the buyer's shoes and slows down to validate and acknowledge the problem. "I can only imagine how frustrating that must be for you. And I am guessing you are receiving lots of phone calls from customers that aren't very pleasant, which makes for long work days." The empathetic salesperson lets the prospect know that she can relate to her situation. She is slow to offer solutions, and quick to listen and validate.

Stephen Covey, author of *The 7 Habits of Highly Effective People* (Free Press, 1990), says, "Most people do not listen with the intent to understand; they listen with the intent to reply."

Empathetic salespeople are tuned in during a sales meeting, with their full focus on the prospect or customers. They aren't thinking about their prior appointment or next appointment. As a result of being fully present, they are keenly aware of all the dynamics in the room, spoken and unspoken.

Case Study

As you read in the Introduction, our colleague, Marty Lassen, is vice president of Complete Intelligence, a business consulting company. She and her partner, Scott Halford, do a lot of work with executives in the field of emotional intelligence.

Marty tells the story of showing up to a meeting with the intention of talking about future business with a large client. Because of Marty's training in emotional intelligence, she immediately picked up on the fact that her client was distracted, not really into the business conversation. Instead of pushing her agenda of gaining more business, Marty closed her notebook and said, "Jim, I get the feeling that our agenda about future training needs isn't top priority for you today. What else is going on that I might be able to help you with?"

Marty read the client correctly and Jim went on to share a family concern. Marty, whose empathy makes her a likeable person, was able to offer some insight and share a few resources that could help Jim solve his most pressing concern that day. No contract was signed. However, a relationship was cemented and Jim is a raving fan of Complete Intelligence.

A Day in the Life of Your Clients and Prospects

Do you really know what your clients' and prospects' lives are like? If you don't, how can you connect on a deeper level? How can you empathize with their challenges and aspirations?

Think about your own personal life and who you like and connect with. Working mothers like to be with other working moms because they can relate to the juggling act of kids and family. Athletes like hanging around other athletes because they can relate to the discipline of getting ready for a race or discuss how to get over a nagging injury. CEO forums are popular because the participants are with like-minded people sharing similar issues and challenges.

Empathy is the ability to see the world from another person's perspective, even if you don't share the same roles, responsibilities, or day-to-day challenges. If you don't know what a day in the life of your prospect is like, it's going to be difficult to connect and build likeability.

Here's the day in the lives of our clients and prospects. With large clients, the directors of sales are stretched because they are always managing up and down. They have pressure from the CEO and CFO to hit numbers while managing the many demands coming in from their sales team. Salespeople are requesting help with closing deals or handling internal operations issues. They put in long weeks flying on airplanes, sleeping in beds with bad pillows, and coming back to the office to piles of reports and emails. They partner with us because they do not have the time to develop training modules or materials.

Our smaller clients and prospects are CEOs who are also the president, sales manager, chief marketing officer, and chief bottle washer. He or she is the main rainmaker and gets frustrated trying to hire and duplicate themselves, wondering why no one wants to work as hard as they do. They are first in and last out, and are tired of burning the candle at both ends. They look to us as a shortcut and partner to establish systems and processes.

If we were to ask you to write a paragraph about your clients and prospects, could you do it? If not, take your best clients out to lunch and conduct interviews. Find out about their daily lives. You cannot relate to that which you know nothing about. And when you can relate, you increase the likeability factor.

Case Study

One of our clients, Ensign Drilling, builds oil rigs and is a successful company that is growing in leaps and bounds and experiencing double-digit growth. There are many reasons for its growth: strategic thinking, state-of-the-art equipment, and good people, among them. There is also another reason: Tom Schledwitz, Senior Vice President, places an emphasis on soft skills, including empathy. Tom wanted his corporate staff to gain a better understanding of its team members in the field, called "roughnecks." These are the men who work on the oil rigs. He noticed the corporate team sometimes got frustrated with lack of quick response or incomplete administrative forms submitted by roughnecks.

To gain perspective for everyone in the company, Tom went to the rigs and interviewed the roughnecks on camera. He asked questions such as:

- ▶ What time does your day start?
- ▶ How long do you work each day?
- ▶ What's important to you?

Tom then held an off-site meeting, where the video was shown to the internal corporate team. Few people in the corporate office knew much about a roughneck's day. They discovered that it often starts at 4:00 A.M. because of a two-hour commute followed by a twelve-hour shift. Many people in the corporate office were touched and surprised to hear the "tough roughnecks" share how important their families were and the difficulty of working on Christmas because rigs can't shut down. The result was a better understanding of their fellow team members and the difficulty in responding quickly when you are working and traveling sixteen hours a day.

The corporate team empathized and changed some systems, processes, and attitudes based on their new insight on the day in the life of a roughneck. Likeability increased between the two teams as a result of "walking a mile in the other person's shoes."

Know, Relate, and Build Likeability

Harvey Mackay is the founder and chairman of the MackayMitchell Envelope Company. He is also bestselling author of *Swim with the Sharks Without Being Eaten Alive* (Ballantine Books, 1996). We guess he scores high in interpersonal skills because of a well-known tool he developed called the Mackay 66. It is a questionnaire designed to help his sales team learn everything about their customers. The questionnaire has sixty-six questions, from personal hobbies to names of kids to political affiliations.

His salespeople fill out this form on every customer. (Do you think his sales team members know about a day in the life of their customers?) This sales team uses interpersonal skills to win business and it seems to work, because MackayMitchell produces 4 billion envelopes every year.

How about you? What do you need to learn about your clients and prospects to increase your likeability? Make it a goal to learn more about a day in their lives.

Enthusiastic or Annoying?

Empathetic salespeople are good at relating to and reading people. The problem is that salespeople still use outdated sales training techniques, which decrease likeability.

Many salespeople have been taught to be enthusiastic. Go into every meeting upbeat and full of energy. Herein lies the problem: Not all of your prospects are enthusiastic, and people buy from people who are like them.

Picture this. A salesperson shows up to meet with the CFO of a large engineering firm. There is a good chance, based on the position and industry, that this CFO is going to be analytical and reserved. The salesperson is bubbly and energetic throughout the meeting because she was taught that enthusiasm is contagious. No, it's not contagious; for some people, it's plain annoying. She is not paying attention and picking up on cues suggesting that the introverted CFO is overwhelmed by the intensity of the meeting. He ends the meeting quickly and potential business is once again lost to chemistry. The salesperson didn't read her prospect and adapt her style of communication.

The empathetic salesperson is aware of their prospect's preferred communication style. She adjusts her style in order to build rapport and likeability by matching and mirroring the prospect's communication style. We've had some people ask us, "If you are adapting your style, aren't you compromising your authenticity?" Our answer is always the same: Our number one goal is to have our prospects and customers comfortable during a meeting. And if that means adapting and adjusting, we are being authentic because of our desire to build a connection.

The skill of matching and mirroring evolved from neurolinguistic programming, an interpersonal communication model that involves the study of language, interpretation, and how we interface and communicate with other people. Co-founders John Bandler and Richard Bandler used their background in linguistics, mathematics, and gestalt therapy to help people learn how to achieve competence and excellence in their personal and professional lives. This approach enhances likeability because you are communicating with your prospects in a manner that aligns with how they think and speak.

For example, if your prospect talks slowly and tends to speak quietly, it's your job to match and mirror her laid-back communication style. We have seen more than one sales call blown in the first five minutes because the salesperson isn't tuned in and speaks loud and fast. This happens frequently during phone conversations when salespeople get nervous and increase their rate of speech. The prospect hangs up, shakes her head, and says, *"I couldn't understand what he was saying."* Translation: The salesperson was not like me and I didn't like the interaction.

Salespeople who pay attention to the dynamics of a sales meeting also match their prospects' and customers' energy level. If you are meeting with a low-key prospect, leave your high-energy self in the car and take your relaxed self to the meeting.

Match and mirror your prospect's body language. If your prospect leans forward, wait about sixty seconds and then gradually lean forward as well. If he crosses his legs, follow his lead, and cross your legs. The prospect starts seeing someone just like him, which is comfortable and likeable.

Another area to adapt and mirror is the type of words your prospect uses during the conversation. People have three major modes for processing information during a sales meeting: visual, auditory, and kinesthetic.

Visuals processors see the world in pictures and use phrases like *"I get the picture,"* *"show me,"* or *"my perspective."* Salespeople who are paying attention use visual words in order to build a connection or make a point: "Let me show you what we have done for other clients" or "Here's the big picture of what we can do for your organization."

Prospects who are auditory process information through listening. You will hear them use phrases like *"I hear you,"* *"sounds like,"* and *"tell me more."* Here's where the disconnect in communication and likeability happens.

The visual salesperson loves to come in with charts and graphs because that's how she processes information. The auditory prospect just wants to listen and doesn't really need to be bothered with a bunch of collateral. The visual keeps shoving information in front of this poor prospect instead of just conducting a conversation. The observant, empathetic salesperson adapts her style to match the prospect's and puts away her visual stuff.

The last style of communication is that of the kinesthetic person. These are prospects who are deliberate in their speech, often slow to answer, and take time to process information. This prospect uses phrases such as, *"I need to get my arms around this,"* *"give me some time to process,"* or *"my gut is telling me."*

This type of prospect is one with whom many salespeople have a hard time connecting because the communication style is so different from their own. In fact, we've decided most salespeople should send the kinesthetic prospect a note of apology after a sales meeting because many get impatient with the slow pace of the meeting. They finish the prospect's and customer's sentences, or their nonverbal communication loudly states, *"Hurry up! I don't have all day for you to sit there and think."*

We once competed with two other training firms for an engagement. We won the project and obviously were pleased. When we asked the owner why he chose us, he replied, *"My gut told me it was a good decision."* Note that his answer didn't include how wonderful he thought our curriculum or solutions were. His answer told us that the ultimate decision was made because we were speaking his language.

Are You Showing Up or Living It Up?

Have you ever been around someone who loves their work? Have you ever been around someone who is just showing up to work, collecting a paycheck? There is quite a difference. You may have heard the phrase, "If you love what you do, you'll never work another day in your life." Salespeople who score high in the emotional intelligence skill of self-actualization are happy people who enjoy their work and are on a journey of personal and professional self-improvement.

They read, listen, and absorb information on how to become a better person and salesperson. It is easy to identify this salesperson in training because he or she is the one who brings case studies for coaching—the one who applies new content immediately.

We find that the best salespeople, the ones already achieving quota, ask for the most coaching because of their desire to improve and reach new heights in their personal and professional development. The late UCLA basketball coach John Wooden said it best: "When you are done learning, you are done."

Self-actualized salespeople provide more value to their prospects and customers because of their continuous learning curve. They bring new ideas, thoughts, and solutions to meetings because they don't settle for "good enough." It's not surprising to learn that salespeople who love their work have customers who love working with them.

On the other hand, there is another group of salespeople called "settlers." Not to be confused with the early pioneers, these sales folks are *not* trying to capture any new frontiers. They have quit learning and settle for "good enough." They settle for average satisfaction from their work. They settle for average commissions. And they settle for showing up in life, not living it up in life.

We have coached hundreds of salespeople and share this piece of advice: If you don't like what you're doing or selling, do your company, your customers, and yourself a favor and get another job. Yes, you can complain about your boss, lack of marketing materials, and a bad territory. But when you look at the data, the common denominator is you—and the fact is, you don't like what you do.

Case Study

Some years ago, a young woman named Brooke contacted us about sales training. She certainly was not our ideal profile as she wasn't in sales; she was an administrative assistant.

Brooke worked at a property and casualty insurance company. She had approached the sales manager several times expressing her desire to enter the sales profession. Unfortunately, the sales manager did not see the potential in Brooke and turned down her requests. She would not settle for "no," so she enrolled in our sales training course and paid for it herself. Brooke turned out to be a star student and eventually quit her job. She landed a sales position with a competitor of her old company and went on to become a top producer at that brokerage firm.

Brooke is a classic example of an individual who scores high in self-actualization. She was on a journey of personal and professional improvement, and took the necessary steps to make her life more fulfilling. Brooke wasn't a settler.

Are You a Joy Giver?

Self-actualized salespeople tend to be joy givers because they are happy in their personal and professional lives. Have you ever noticed that happy people are more likeable than unhappy people?

There is a great scene about this concept from the movie. *The Bucket List*. Morgan Freeman and Jack Nicholson are sitting atop one of the Egyptian pyramids, having a philosophical conversation about life. Freeman shares the ancient Egyptians' beliefs about their entrance into heaven. The Egyptians would first be asked two questions:

1. Have you found joy in your life?
2. Has your life brought joy to others?

The questions shake up Nicholson's character, as relationships and interpersonal skills have not been his strong suit in life. It's a profound scene, and the questions are good ones to ask each day as we interact with clients, prospects, and peers.

As a former vice president of sales, I know firsthand how giving joy affects sales results. Missy Price was a member of my sales team and was a superstar. She was a hard worker, good salesperson—and she was a joy giver. Missy had this huge smile and equally huge heart. She was kind to customer service, even when things got stressful due to missed ship dates. She helped fellow team members with encouragement and support, even when she had a full schedule. Missy's clients did business with her for both her sales acumen as well as her joy-giving attitude. Got joy?

Tim Sanders, author of *The Likeability Factor* (Crown, 2005), shares in his book four traits that likeable people possess: friendliness, relevance, empathy, and realness. Here are a few questions to ask yourself to measure your likeability:

> **Friendliness:** Are you approachable? Do you smile and engage others? Are you interested in other people's personal and professional lives?

> **Relevance:** Who have you helped in the last month? What have you done to help another person? Are you a giver or a taker?

> **Empathy:** Do you work at trying to understand other people's perspectives? Do you listen more than you speak?

> **Realness:** Are you authentic and sincere? Do you show up as the real deal?

Which of these do you score high in? What could you do to increase your likeability factor?

Action Steps for Improving Your Likeability

As the chapter title reads, people buy from people they like and who are like them. Most people think that a salesperson has to be an over-the-top extrovert in order to be likeable. We hope you've gained some insights on other ways to become likeable beyond pure personality style. The good news about this soft skill is that it can be improved with focus, commitment, and practice. There are three steps you can take that will improve your likeability and sales results:

1. Examine your self-regard to see if you are showing up confident, relaxed, and authentic.
2. Create your own Mackay 66.
3. Show up and live it up.

Step #1: Examine Your Self-Regard to See If You Are Showing Up Confident, Relaxed, and Authentic

Ask yourself these questions:

▶ Am I taking myself to the meeting or is my alter ego showing up?

▶ Am I showing up at meetings prepared or nervous?

▶ Where am I taking myself too seriously?

▶ Am I willing to acknowledge and poke fun at my mistakes and shortcomings?

▶ Am I self-focused or other-focused?

Salespeople who are comfortable with themselves have the ability to separate what they do for a living from who they are. They know that success or failure does not define their self-worth because success or failure is more about their roles in life, not their character. And this is true for you, too.

If you fail to close a sale, it does not reflect on your worth as a human being. If you win a sale, it does not raise your worth as a human being. A win or loss should roll off your shoulders rather than into your head, where self-doubt and arrogance can take hold.

Step #2: Create Your Own Mackay 66

Make a commitment to learn more about your customers in order to better relate to them and build relationships. Download this form, www.harveymackay.com/pdfs/mackay66.pdf, or develop your own questions that will help you be more empathetic to your prospect's and customers' needs. Set a goal to interview your current clients in order to learn about a day in their lives. The information might surprise you, and it will help you to better serve your clients.

Once you gain new information, do something with it. People often say knowledge is power. We disagree. Knowledge is power only when it is used and applied.

Step #3: Show Up and Live It Up

Go to YouTube and download the commencement address given by the late Steve Jobs to the 2005 graduating class of Stanford University. In his address, he stresses the importance of going after your dreams and not living your life for other people. Jobs is really talking about self-actualization and pursuing your full potential.

Find purpose in your work and you will find happiness. Years ago, a colleague of mine worked with city bus drivers. Many had "settled" and did not see any real purpose in their work.

Then my colleague got them thinking about the importance of their job. They drove people to work that didn't own cars. These drivers took sick people to the doctor's office. City bus drivers provided transportation for people to visit parents and loved ones. Once the drivers saw the importance of their work, their happiness and job satisfaction increased.

As a sales professional, do you see purpose and value in your position? Do you see how you are helping people every day? You sell services that help businesses grow and keep people employed. Some of you sell products that save lives. Others provide great service that make your customer's day easier and more productive.

One of the best phone calls or emails we can receive at our office is from a client that used one of our tactics or strategies, saying, "It worked. I have a new client." Or, "I am going on the company incentive trip and your training was part of my success." We have a tremendous desire to help our clients. As a result, our work is not really work, because we get such a kick out of teaching, coaching, and mentoring.

Improve your likeability by liking and accepting yourself. Get to know the day in the life of your clients and prospects. Make it all about them. Set personal and professional goals that make you happy and fulfilled—because a happy salesperson is a likeable salesperson.

CHAPTER 5

Expectations

You Get What You Expect

HAVE YOU EVER BEEN a victim of chase mode? This is where the prospect is not returning your phone call after a first meeting or review of a proposal? Have you ever had a sales meeting with a prospect who isn't engaging in the conversation, and you felt like you were talking to yourself? Have you ever showed up to a meeting, expecting the decision makers to be there, but the only people showing up were non–decision makers? How about clients who are constantly dissatisfied with your services because *they* aren't doing what is needed in order to execute and hit deadlines?

Salespeople get upset with prospects and customers because of the above selling scenarios. There's no need to get upset with your prospects or customers. There is a need, however, to take a look at yourself and determine how good you are at setting and managing expectations for a successful business relationship. You get what you expect—and there is a good chance you didn't set expectations for dealing with decision making and client satisfaction or eliminating chase mode and one-sided sales conversations.

The ability to effectively manage expectations—both our own and our prospects and clients'—is an integral part of any sales professional's success. It's a skill that must be incorporated throughout the entire sales process. Clear expectations define how you and your prospects and customers will do business. Managing expectations includes agreeing to how you will treat each other during a meeting, the roles and responsibilities of each person involved, and the next steps each person will take to achieve mutual goals.

Most salespeople have been taught to have a clear purpose or objective for a meeting. What they have not been taught is how to set expectations for a collaborative conversation. Many salespeople go into meetings as a subordinate rather than as a qualified peer. The result is the frustrating selling scenarios mentioned in the first paragraph of this chapter.

Expectation management is especially important at the start of a business relationship. You get what you expect—and top salespeople expect to be treated with respect and as a peer. How you set and manage expectations at this point often determines whether you will be treated as a valued partner or just a vendor.

Vendor relationships are those in which the prospect or customer really doesn't care about you or the relationship, but cares only about price. When you meet with this type of person, he isn't willing to engage in a conversation and gives short, guarded answers to questions, refusing to participate in a consultative meeting. As a client, he is often the type that, each year, will newly bid the work you have been doing for them over the past year, even after you have delivered excellent quality and service. He believes in win-lose negotiations and is a high-maintenance client who has little respect for the profession of sales.

Partners, on the other hand, respect a salesperson's expertise and are willing to pay for value. Customers and prospects who believe in partnerships treat salespeople with respect. They are willing to participate in a dialogue and are open about sharing concerns and goals. They don't play games and believe that a win-win philosophy for both parties is necessary to conduct long-term, profitable business.

Good salespeople excel at setting and managing expectations for what they need to conduct business. While there are hard selling skills necessary to set and manage expectations, we find that soft skills such as assertiveness, reality testing, problem solving, empathy, and self-regard are equally important in initiating and maintaining a partnership rather than a vendor relationship. Let's take a look at the soft skills needed to create peer-to-peer conversations rather than superficial sales dialogues.

Partnership or Vendor-ship?

Effective salespeople are good at disqualifying prospects from the outset who treat them like vendors. They quickly send these time-wasters to their competitor and invest their energy in prospects and clients who believe in partnering. They are masters at setting up a collaborative relationship from the moment they contact a prospect to set a first appointment.

Managing expectations sounds easy until emotions get in the way. Too many salespeople get excited and are just happy to get the appointment. They say things like, *"Virginia, I know how busy you are. I will just need twenty minutes of your time to go over our products and services."* Reread that sentence and note the poor expectations being set by the salesperson. He sounds apologetic even asking for a meeting. The statement is not setting the expectation for a peer-to-peer conversation. Asking for "just twenty minutes" is certainly not setting the tone for a consultative sales meeting. It is setting the expectation for a product dump meeting and a vendor relationship.

Salespeople good at managing expectations are assertive and possess good self-regard, comfortably stating what they need. They value their time and know from experience that if a prospect is not willing to invest time in discussing challenges, he's not a likely customer. They set expectations for a dialogue, not a monologue; they aim for a partner meeting rather than a vendor meeting. They might set appointments this way:

> "Virginia, I think there are some things my company might be able to help you with. In order for us to explore whether we have some solutions for your company, we will need about an hour to discuss your challenges and goals. I don't want to assume to know how these challenges are affecting your business, so I will be asking a number of questions to better understand your specific situation. Will that work for you?"

Notice the difference in how this salesperson set and managed expectations in comparison to the first example. Expectations were set about the time needed to diagnose challenges. The salesperson let the prospect clearly know that the meeting was going to be a dialogue, not a one-way monologue and sales pitch.

In addition to setting the time parameters of the meeting, effective and assertive salespeople also ensure that their prospects understand who they expect to attend the meeting.

We've heard more than one war story from sales reps who set up a meeting with the understanding that a key decision maker in the company needed to attend, only to arrive and find out the key decision maker is unable to make the meeting. The salesperson is left in that uncomfortable and unprofitable place of meeting a non–decision maker who could say no but not say yes.

These nonproductive meetings can be avoided if you are specific and clear about your expectations for who needs to attend the meeting. This type of conversation also qualifies how serious your prospect is about solving an issue or challenge. Decision makers show up to meetings when they are committed to changing or improving.

What's Your Mindset?

So far, we have been talking about creating a mindset in a prospect that allows for a successful first encounter. We've been focusing on managing the client's point of view. But what about your own mindset? Managing your own expectations about a meeting is an equally important part of a successful business relationship.

Too many salespeople go into a sales meeting with the wrong intention: to close business. They throw out trial closes such as, "Wouldn't you agree?" or "If we could, would you want to?" If you are trying to set up a partnership rather than a vendor relationship, act like a partner, not a typical salesperson.

We teach our clients to go into a sales meeting with a different intent: to seek the truth and do the right thing. Lose the attachment to the outcome of the meeting and get comfortable with hearing either a yes *or* a no.

This concept came to us from an unusual place: the district attorney's office. I am married to a career prosecutor, a *Law and Order*–type guy. Prior to meeting Jim, I didn't know too much about this type of law. So on one of our first dates, I asked him if he made a lot of money if he won a case. Jim looked puzzled and replied, "No we are held to a different code of ethics in my profession. We are charged with seeking the truth and doing the right thing."

Because of this code of ethics, Jim is not attached to any one outcome. He *is* attached to finding the truth and evidence behind each case that ends up on his desk. His intent is to remain objective and ask a lot of tough questions: "Why was the stop made?" "What makes you think the defendant is guilty?" "Where's the proof?" "How do we know for sure?"

Seeking the truth during sales meetings should be the goal of every salesperson. Ask questions and come to a solution that makes the most sense for the customer, rather than simply try to land a deal and hit your quota. And the reality is, sometimes the right solution has nothing to do with your product or service.

When you are attached to the outcome of a sale, you avoid asking the tough questions such as, "Do you really need to do anything?" You are attached to hearing a yes, not the truth. Think like a prosecutor. What questions would you ask your prospects if you were simply investigating their business case, hoping to understand the truth of their situation, rather than trying to arrive at the desired result?

When you lose the attachment to the outcome of a meeting, you focus on uncovering objective data rather than what you'd like to hear. The emotional intelligence skill of reality testing is important in having an objective mindset. Rather than asking questions that try to get you the answers you want to hear, such as *"If we could save you time in your day, would that be of interest?"*, reality testing helps you ask smart questions that test the data, such as *"Are you sure this particular challenge is costing you loss of time? Is there something else happening at the company that is contributing to this time problem?"*

Seeking the truth by having the right mindset creates a peer-to-peer conversation because the prospect isn't being manipulated by obvious leading questions. You're acting like a partner, not a vendor.

Are You Still Trying to Overcome Objections?

This new mindset might mean letting go of old axioms you have no doubt heard. Many salespeople are still taught archaic sales techniques for overcoming a prospect's objections. They are told: "The first objection is never the real one." "A no gets you closer to a yes." "Don't give up unless you have overcome the objection three to five times."

Is any prospect in their right mind going to bring up an objection, knowing that you have been trained to overcome it and not take no for an answer? Instead of being open and honest, the prospect avoids bringing up real concerns. Needless to say, this mentality doesn't do a lot for creating a partnership or a relationship. It also gets a lot of salespeople into chase mode, where they end up pursuing a customer who is not interested.

Here's a novel idea. Don't overcome the objections—ask questions that will *bring them up*. Conduct this exercise with yourself or with your sales team. Write down all the reasons a prospect doesn't move forward with you. Here are the typical objections our clients hear from prospects:

➤ They believe it will be a hassle to switch vendors.

➤ Your company is not as well branded as the competition.

➤ They can possibly do the work internally instead of outsourcing it.

➤ They have a very limited budget.

➤ The timing is bad.

➤ They have an existing vendor relationship.

Ask yourself when you would like to find out about these objections: *before* or *after* you spend time writing a proposal? Of course, most salespeople answer that they would prefer to uncover deal breakers before writing a proposal. Now ask yourself the next question, when *do* you find out about these objections—before or after writing a proposal? Fifty percent of the time, the answer we hear from salespeople is that they find out after writing a proposal. Wow, what a waste of time!

Many salespeople initially push back on this concept, fearing that bringing up an objection will plant a seed of doubt in the prospect's mind or a reason not to do business. But here's a sales tip: your prospect has already thought about all the objections. That's why you keep running into these objections too late in the sales process, after you've submitted a proposal. You'll close more business if you bring up an objection because you will be present to facilitate a conversation regarding concerns and misperceptions.

Keep in mind that you are setting the expectation for a partnership. This requires real-world dialogue, not superficial conversation. Put on your empathy hat and step into your prospect's shoes. Ask questions about potential problems or stalls:

➤ *"Joan, since this is a fairly new product, I am guessing you might be wondering about reliability. Should we talk about this?"*

➤ *"Joan, you haven't brought this up, so I don't know if it's an issue for you. Our firm is a small boutique firm and I know you are looking at some larger firms. Are there any concerns about our capability to deliver the same quality of work?"*

➤ *"Joan, you shared with me that you had a bad experience with our company five years ago. I am guessing you might be wondering if we have corrected some of those customer service issues or not. Should we talk about that?"*

Don't overcome the objections: bring them up. Creating this kind of exchange will serve you well in the long run. You will be able to ask and answer questions regarding their objections, acting as an advisor, not a self-centered salesperson. To do this, it's critical that you shift your expectations; understand that you are on an investigative, fact-finding mission rather than a close-the-deal-now mission. That is a partner mindset.

Case Study

One of our innovation clients, Imaginibbles, is very good at managing expectations and discussing potential problems before writing a proposal. As a result, they don't waste time with unqualified opportunities. If Imaginibbles loses, they like to lose early in the sales process.

Their target market is Fortune 500 companies that often have internal research and development departments. Part of Imaginibbles' service offering includes new product development and customer research. Many of their prospects have internal teams charged with similar responsibilities. So the obvious objection is, "Why should we hire you?" Part of their qualification process is figuring out if the prospect believes in outsourcing or if they are "do-it-yourself-ers."

At some point, before any proposal, the Imaginibbles team brings up the potential objection: *"Mike, we appreciate your interest and willingness to take at look at the work we have done in innovation and strategy. But we are curious—what is making you take a look at outsourcing this when you have a ton of talent on staff?"*

Because they aren't attached to the outcome of the sale, they ask the tough question and are willing to hear the truth, which could be a no. Qualified prospects immediately share common reasons for outsourcing: the internal team is overworked; there is worry about groupthink; or they sincerely believe outside perspective and collaboration helps create better products.

Unqualified prospects decide to do the work with just their internal team. The good news is that Imaginibbles did not waste time writing a practice proposal for a nonqualified opportunity.

Managing expectations and dealing with the potential problem paid off nicely for Imaginibbles, which recently landed a six-figure contract with a company that had a substantial internal research and development department. The owner attributes part of their success to seeking the truth and dealing with potential problems early in the sales process.

Does the Prospect Deserve a Second Meeting?

Once you have explored all of these issues in an initial conversation, the next step is to evaluate the need for another appointment. Salespeople get excited when prospects agree to a second meeting. And because of their desire to close a deal, they often fail to ask the tough question and apply their reality-testing skills: Is there really a need for another meeting or even a follow-up call? Did they hear any "pain" during the first meeting? Enough pain to justify writing a proposal and scheduling another meeting to present?

Don't let excitement and poor emotion management override your objective thinking. Before agreeing to a second meeting, often based only on the slim hope that you might make a sale, test the reality of the situation. Ask yourself some truth-seeking questions:

> ► Did your client express a real problem that needs solving in the first meeting? (*If you didn't hear any pain during that meeting, why are you meeting with the prospect again? Are you headed down the path of writing a practice proposal?*)

> ► Is the prospect open to sharing his budget? (*If the prospect is unwilling to share his budget, why do you want to keep working with a noncollaborative person? Does this match your expectations for being treated like a partner?*)

> ► Is the prospect willing to set up introductions to other decision makers? (*If the prospect isn't willing to involve other decision makers, aren't you headed toward an ineffective recommendation? Another practice proposal? Does this look like collaboration?*)

Asking yourself these questions will save you many headaches and much time chasing a prospect who doesn't need your services or isn't willing to engage in a collaborative relationship.

A common example of not setting and managing expectations for the follow-up meeting or call often occurs at trade shows. Sales reps return back to the office, excited about their new contacts, only to end up in email and voicemail hell. Companies spend thousands of dollars on exhibits, promotional items, and travel but invest little time and money in training their sales team in how to set and manage their own expectations, as well as those of potential customers.

For example, a prospect comes to your booth and asks, "What do you guys do?" You and the prospect have a short conversation. The prospect states that he is very interested, and you agree to follow up with the prospect after the show. You honor your part of the agreement and call the prospect. Then you email. Next, you call the prospect again. Yes, chase mode is in full play. In this selling situation, chase mode occurred for one main reason. You didn't set clear expectations for specific next steps or deal with potential problems up front.

Here's an example of properly setting expectations and establishing a partnership not a vendor-ship.

> "Now George, we all know what these trade shows are like. You're going to get back to your office and have a to-do list a mile long. When do you suggest I call? And you're going to get bombarded with calls from other vendors. What should I say or send ahead of time to remind you of our conversation? By the way, if you change your mind, would you please accept my call, even if it's only to tell me no? That way I won't become a sales stalker after this show."

Notice how many expectations are being set by the salesperson to be discussed and agreed upon by both the salesperson and the prospect before the salesperson is willing to invest her valuable time. Also note that successful salespeople seek the truth by pointing out potential problems before they occur. It prevents chase mode and bad knees, both of which come from running after too many uninterested prospects!

Be assertive and state what you need nicely. It makes sales a lot easier and more comfortable for both the salesperson and the prospect.

Set and Manage Expectations to Create Raving Fans

As the business relationship evolves, it is your job to continue to let clients know what you expect of them. There is an old saying in business: "The customer is always right." Salespeople jump through hoops trying to please the customer. And sometimes their hoop jumping doesn't pay off because expectations for success were not set, agreed upon, or managed throughout the sales process and client engagement.

Here's one scenario that you might be able to relate to. The deal is closed and the salesperson is happy with her new customer. Project implementation is about to begin, with the goal of completing by the end of the quarter. The salesperson starts experiencing problems in getting meetings set up with key stakeholders. These meetings are necessary to keep the project moving forward and hitting agreed-upon deadlines. The salesperson pushes and cajoles the client, trying to hold meetings and gather the necessary data, with little success. The deadline is missed and the client shares her disappointment about the ineffectiveness of the salesperson and his company. The salesperson has an unhappy customer, but not because his company fell short of expectations. The client is actually the one that fell short and doesn't own up to it because expectations for success were not set before the project started.

Setting and managing expectations requires discussing each company's role in achieving successful outcomes. It means discussing expectations regarding potential problems—before they occur. This is a key principle in expectation management. The expectation must be set before the selling event.

Here are some questions you might ask in order to firm up the rules of the partnership and each person's role in successful outcomes:

▶ Is the customer going to be okay moving the deadline out by two weeks if their internal team falls short of expectations?

▶ What happens if key stakeholders miss meetings?

▶ What should we do if critical information isn't getting transferred to us?

▶ Who is accountable for this project on the client's end?

Be assertive and set expectations with your new and old customers regarding their role in a successful outcome. Good business results happen when companies work together as partners. And partnership thinking comes from setting and managing expectations for success.

Case Study

We worked with a website development firm whose staff was very frustrated. The account managers were becoming expert "hoop jumpers." They were trying very hard to create raving fans and, instead, often ended up with unsatisfied clients. Many of their clients were small and didn't have a full-time marketing person on staff. Pictures, information, and marketing copy were often delayed getting to the developers, which pushed back the launch date of the new website.

We worked with this team and helped them set and manage expectations about each company's responsibility in ensuring success in the design and implementation of the website. Roles, responsibilities, and potential problems were openly and thoroughly discussed. The website development firm found that its clients appreciated the clarity and, as a result, did a better job of working as a partner to achieve successful outcomes. There was less finger-pointing and blaming because most issues had already been discussed and agreed upon before any work was started on a customer's new website.

Customer satisfaction increased because expectations were set early in the process and managed throughout the development of the website. The company is now well on its way to producing raving fans and the hoops have been put away in storage.

Soft skills needed to create raving fans are problem solving and assertiveness. Analyze when, where, and how client dissatisfaction occurs. Be accountable and accept where you and your company fall short. State what you need from the customers in order to provide exceptional results. Business is a two-way street. Make sure you and your customers are driving in the right direction.

Action Steps for Improving the Way You Manage Expectations

Make it a goal to get very good at setting clear expectations. Develop a mindset for partnerships not vendor-ships. The first leads to profits, the second leads to price chopping and practice proposals.

Eliminate vague or fuzzy agreements. They aren't beneficial to you or to the prospect. When you and your prospect are on the same page, time is invested wisely and outcomes for mutual success are defined and agreed upon. Then you have something called a partnership.

Here are some action steps that will help you get what you expect:

1. Review your last three months of sales appointments and analyze how you showed up.

2. Visualize and practice setting and managing expectations.

3. Revisit the value you bring to your prospects and clients.

Step #1: Review Your Last Three Months of Sales Appointments and Analyze How You Showed Up

Were you assertive, stating nicely what you needed in order to conduct effective business, or did you slip into passive sales behavior — going along to get along? If you were passive, what was the trigger that set off such a response?

For example, does the following scenario sound all too familiar? You schedule a first appointment with a prospect and he agrees to a forty-five-minute meeting. But when you sit down and double-check the time expectation with the prospect, he says he only has about fifteen minutes.

You let your emotions get the best of you and go into fight-or-flight mode, panicking and moving into a product dump because in your mind there is no time to ask questions and run a consultative sales call.

If this experience is common to you, think about a more productive response to this situation. Recognize that if you simply go ahead with the meeting under the new time constraint, the conversation is likely to be one-sided, boring, and will probably end with the prospect telling you he needs to think your offer over.

Instead, change your response by managing your emotions. Tap into your empathy and recognize that a first sales meeting can be a little uncomfortable for the prospect. He is probably worried that you are meeting with him with the sole intention of selling him something he doesn't need. Don't react to his remark that he only has fifteen minutes. Instead, reset expectations for a consultative meeting: *"Mr. Prospect, we can do one of two things. I don't know how much we will cover in fifteen minutes but we can get started and at the end of that time determine whether a second meeting makes sense. Or should we reschedule? It looks like you might have some other fires to attend to."*

By being assertive and empathetic, you reset the prospect's expectations for a successful meeting and also state the truth: you can't get much done in fifteen minutes. We've found in almost every selling situation, the prospect agrees to get started and the meeting ends up running for forty-five minutes or longer as initially agreed upon.

Good prospects are not offended by a salesperson setting expectations. The key word here is "good." Good prospects respect you and what you bring to the sales table. Good prospects understand and value partnerships and, therefore, treat you like a partner. Think of how often you have fallen short of this mindset over the past months and commit to a different approach.

Step #2: Visualize and Practice Setting and Managing Expectations

Once you've committed to the idea of controlling expectations on all sides, work on forming those new neural pathways in your brain to change your normal, ineffective responses. Think about recent selling scenarios where you were passive and didn't state what you needed. What was the outcome of those meetings? Did you end up in chase mode? Did you write an ineffective proposal because you got rushed during the interview?

Work on your assertiveness to prevent victim mentality. Salespeople who aren't assertive turn into sales doormats. They complain that they are always being taken advantage of, which creates resentment and an inability to enjoy their job. Apply some reality testing. Is the prospect or customer taking advantage of you or are you just not asking for what you need?

In order to practice becoming more assertive, identify non-threatening environments where you can practice different responses to difficult situations. For example, if you lack assertiveness, you might be one of those people reluctant to send cold food back in a restaurant. Instead of enduring a bad meal, smile at the waiter and ask him to reheat your food. Small acts of assertiveness help you get better at developing this skill.

Step #3: Revisit the Value You Bring to Your Prospects and Clients

A successful business transaction is mutually beneficial for both the salesperson and customer. If you find yourself being treated like a vendor, remind yourself of the value you bring to your customers. If you don't believe in your value, why should your customer? Make a list of all the ways your product or service helps your customers. For example:

- ▶ Your service improves profitability by eliminating ineffective processes.
- ▶ Your product frees people up to work on higher-priority items.
- ▶ You help keep your customers competitive in a global market.
- ▶ You help your customer look better to their customers, which in turn helps them retain their best clients.
- ▶ You are a shortcut and can help companies ramp up without wasting precious time.
- ▶ Your quick response time prevents downtime for your clients.

These are a few areas where sales professionals help their clients. Make your own list because it will remind you not to shortchange yourself on what to expect from a sales meeting and a business transaction. Look at the list often to build your confidence and self-regard. You are a valuable resource to your prospects and clients. Don't ever doubt it or forget it.

Set and manage expectations early and often during the sales process. Remember, you get what you expect. Do you go into appointments expecting to be treated as a peer and professional? Or do you show up as a subservient salesperson, just hoping to get some time and attention? Show up expecting to be treated like a partner, not a vendor.

Follow popular TV talk show host Dr. Phil's advice: "We teach people how to treat us. Own, rather than complain about, how people treat you. Learn to renegotiate the relationships to have what you want."

CHAPTER 6

Questioning Skills

What's Your Prospect's Story?

SALES PROFESSIONALS often use the phrase, "Find the prospect's pain." The idea is that if the salesperson can uncover the prospect's business challenges, there is a much greater chance of the prospect writing them a check to resolve them.

Studies support that point of view. Neil Rackham, author of bestselling books such as *SPIN Selling* (McGraw-Hill, 1988) and *Major Account Selling* (McGraw-Hill, 1989), has done extensive research on why prospects buy. His investigation shows that close ratios increase as much as 50 percent when salespeople discover the prospect's pain and then discuss its impact or implications with the prospect.

There are also hundreds of sales books, blogs, and articles that teach salespeople to ask questions and probe in order to find this thing called "pain." So we go back to some age-old questions: Why do so many salespeople launch into presenting solutions too soon and too often before asking enough questions to diagnose the root cause of the prospect's problem? Why are salespeople more interested in telling their story than in learning their prospect's story?

Many of us have seen this preference in action, having either witnessed or been the victim of a "verbal assault" from a salesperson upon the first mention of a business challenge. This is when the salesperson moves into "sales attack" mode. She does little or no probing to learn the prospect's story. She does not ask enough questions to understand how the problem is affecting the prospect. She does, however, do a lot of product dumping and pitching. The prospect—"the victim"—gets stuck hearing another canned and premature sales pitch that doesn't address his real concerns.

When the prospect is unable to get any satisfaction from meeting with the salesperson, he moves on to try to conduct his due diligence with two other salespeople. Unfortunately, they have all graduated from the same school of selling: SAU, Sales Attack University. Everyone looks and sounds the same. Each salesperson adamantly asserts that his or her company offers the best quality, service, and expertise. And each salesperson assures the prospect that their company is all about relationships and customer care. How is a prospect supposed to choose? The only real differentiator seems to be price, so the prospect buys from the low-price provider.

The salesperson who loses then complains to her sales manager or CEO: "If we had better pricing, I could win more business." Some companies accept this excuse and lower their prices, only to discover that cheaper pricing doesn't help close more business. It only takes first place in the race to zero margins. Other companies focus only on selling skills. (Yes, you know where we are headed.) They review the importance of asking questions and throw out lots of tired rhetoric such as, "God gave you two ears and one mouth for a reason." Salespeople nod in agreement and commit to do what seems fairly simple: ask questions, talk less, and listen more.

The above approaches are well intended, but they are ineffective because they don't get to the bottom of why salespeople aren't asking enough questions and are offering solutions too soon.

Emotional intelligence skills such as impulse control, emotional self-awareness, problem solving, and empathy can play a huge role in conducting a consultative, value-driven sales meeting that will uncover a prospect's true pain. Let's take a closer look at how these skills help salespeople ask more questions, learn their prospect's story, and eliminate premature solutions.

Listen Before You Leap

Impulse control is an emotional intelligence skill that affects a salesperson's ability to ask questions *and* listen to the answers. It's the ability to resist or delay an impulse or temptation to act. A successful salesperson possesses good impulse control. He patiently asks qualifying questions and tough questions. He's not in a hurry to show the prospect how smart he is by offering up solutions too early in the sales process.

Together, he and the prospect identify the problem, discuss its implications, and commit to fixing the challenge. He is good at listening before he leaps. As a result, he is closing business at full margin because he has invested the time to uncover the key decision criteria.

Salespeople who don't fit this description tend to leap before they listen. They are impatient. When a prospect shares a problem, the low-impulse-control salesperson puts on her solution cape and leaps into prescribing fixes. This isn't her first time hearing this particular problem, and since her company helps clients solve the same or similar issues every day, she invests little time—and sometimes no time at all—in asking questions that can uncover the financial and strategic impact of the problem to the prospect and/or the organization.

The ability to control our impulse to present solutions is linked to our emotional self-awareness. Salespeople who take time to reflect and review their actions during a sales meeting may discover they are falling into the common trap of "buying the buying signal." Many salespeople are coached to listen for buying signals. These signals are pains that a prospect shares with the salesperson during a meeting. The problem is that salespeople get excited. They "buy the buying signal" without any evidence that the prospect's problem is real enough or big enough to fix. They aren't ever sure if the prospect is committed to investing time and money in making necessary changes.

Use the "3Ws" Formula

When prospects make statements like, "We need to fix this service problem" or "We've got to improve in order to stay ahead of our competitors," they open the door for us to allow our emotions to take over. It's easy to get sloppy executing our sales process. We don't ask enough questions, the right questions, or the tough questions. In order to stop our clients from "buying the buying" signal, we teach them how to use the 3Ws formula. When a prospect shares a pain or problem, you can slow yourself down by asking the following questions.

The First W: WHY

The first question to ask is: *Why* is this a problem? You probably don't know. You may be able to guess based on meetings with other prospects, but that's all you are doing. You can make assumptions, but that is not an effective approach to closing business. For example, in our business, a prospect might share with us that she is having trouble finding good salespeople. That statement doesn't tell us why selection and hiring is a problem. Is turnover costing her business? Does she need to grow the company to attract investors? Each prospect's "why" is different even though the problem sounds the same.

The Second W: WHAT?

The next question attempts to uncover the current impact of the problem. *What* is the impact to the organization? Is the company losing customers? Is this problem affecting the company's reputation? Is the company spending too many hours paying staff overtime in an effort to address the problem? There are specific answers you want to uncover by asking *specific* impact questions such as: What is the *financial impact* to the prospect? (How much is this problem costing the customer?) What is the *strategic impact* to the prospect? (Are they unable to grow in a particular niche? Is the problem affecting global expansion?) And what is the *personal impact*? (Is your prospect under increasing scrutiny to perform? Is her job in jeopardy?)

When you uncover the answers to these questions, price-shopping conversations begin to go away because you help the prospect discover the cost of doing business as usual or doing nothing.

The Third W: WHAT?

The third question is also a what?—and it carries the previous "what?"s to a new (and possibly not-thought-about) level. An impact question with spin! What is the *future impact* for this prospect if they *don't* solve this problem? Will it get bigger? How much bigger will it be a year from now? Will it become the problem that brings them down?

Here's a short example of using the 3Ws sales approach.

PROSPECT: *"We need to get more aggressive with our marketing strategy because we're losing business to our competition."*

SALESPERSON: *"That has to be frustrating. What's not working with your current marketing? What's not happening that you'd like to see happen?"* (WHY is their marketing strategy a problem?)

PROSPECT: *"Well, we're generating plenty of opportunities. They're just the wrong type of opportunities."*

SALESPERSON: *"What is it costing your organization by not attracting the right type of prospects? Are you selling smaller deals? Are you being forced to lower your prices because you're not attracting prospects that buy on value?"* (WHAT is the financial impact of this problem?)

PROSPECT: *"We're actually selling large deals. The problem is that they are sold at low margin. We need at least a 30 percent margin and we're closer to 15 percent."*

SALESPERSON: *"What happens if you* don't *address this issue?"* (WHAT is the future impact to your company if you decide to live with the status quo?)

PROSPECT: *"We're going to have to lay off people and I don't want to do that. I have some great people working here. Layoffs would also force me to work even longer hours than I already am."* (Personal impact is uncovered.)

The 3Ws formula helps you ask questions that define the real problem and the associated implications of not solving it. The process makes your prospects think through their unique needs and answer tough questions that don't necessarily have easy answers. Control your impulse to tell and solve. Ask more and talk less.

Case Study

One of our IT consulting clients did a good job applying the 3Ws formula. When our client met with the CIO of a rapidly growing firm, they first discussed the various problems his IT department was facing, one of which was that highly paid personnel were buried handling the day-to-day minutia of employees' complaints.

It would have been easy for the sales team to assume to know why this was an issue. Instead of assuming, however, they asked the CIO to explain why this issue was a problem for him. He explained that his team wasn't getting to the "whiteboard" projects, the strategic projects. Once they understood the CIO's why, the team asked impact questions that helped the CIO recognize the financial impact of the problem. Together, they calculated the number of hours being spent each month on internal issues and the associated payroll costs. Finally, questions were asked around future pain. What will happen to his organization if strategic initiatives continue to be ignored because his team is always in firefighting mode? The prospect came to the realization that the company would lose clients and fall behind their competitors, seriously compromising their ability to attract and close new opportunities.

The 3Ws formula paid off as the CIO made the decision to outsource some of his IT functions to my client, landing them a $250,000 project.

Make Your Prospect's Brain Hurt

Several years ago, a client of mine called me and asked if I could facilitate an offsite retreat. I decided, based on the client's retreat objectives, that a facilitator who specialized in strategic management consulting would be a better choice. I referred my client to one of my colleagues and followed up with her a few days later to ask how the appointment had gone. There was a long pause (which is never a good sign), after which she replied, "It was fine." But upon further questioning, she shared her disappointment:

"Colleen, I don't mind meeting with salespeople and consultants. However, I do mind wasting my time. When I meet with someone, I expect the person to ask good questions. The type of questions that make my brain hurt. Your colleague did neither." Needless to say, my colleague wasn't hired.

My client summed up nicely what busy prospects are looking for in salespeople and consultants. They want their thinking and the way they do business challenged. They have enough "yes" people in their lives and don't want or need another run-of-the-mill, safe, howdy meeting.

Here are a few other questions, in addition to the 3Ws, that might help you conduct hurt-my-brain conversations:

- ► Who loses their job if this problem doesn't go away?

- ► Are you looking for a quick fix or a game changer?

- ► If you lose market share, how tough is it going to be to win it back from your competitor?

- ► What is the cost of doing nothing? Is your biggest competitor sitting back doing nothing or are they getting more aggressive?

- ► Who's going to get in the way of the change that needs to happen?

- ► How would you rate your organization on accountability and execution?

Good salespeople make their prospects think and look at their business issues in a different light. They don't worry about asking the tough questions because they know good prospects appreciate salespeople that make their brains hurt.

Get to the Real Pain

The profession of sales involves a lot of psychology. Psychologists are trained to recognize that a problem presented by a patient is usually not the real problem. For example, a person sets an appointment with a psychologist because he is depressed. That is the *presenting* problem, but it's not the real issue.

Once the psychologist starts asking questions, she and the patient discover that the depression is caused by the patient's inability to deal with conflict. Now that the psychologist knows the real problem, she can work on the right solution: improving her patient's conflict management skills.

The same scenario occurs in sales. The problem presented by your prospect is often not the real problem. Good salespeople recognize this and apply their problem-solving skills to uncover the real issue. Problem solving is the ability to find solutions to problems where emotions are involved. (And if you are calling on a prospect with a real challenge, there is emotion associated with the issue.) It requires being disciplined and methodical in asking good questions and smart questions instead of letting your emotions take over and start presenting solutions too soon. This disciplined approach of asking questions helps you look at the "presenting problem" from all angles in order to diagnose the real pain.

Then, when it does come time to make a recommendation, your solution is right on target because you took the time to uncover the real issues and challenges.

Here's an example from our business. We often hear, "My sales team is not prospecting. We need help." It would be very easy for us to ask a few questions and go into solution mode. Instead, we move beyond the presenting problem, apply our problem-solving skills, and ask three questions to uncover the *real* "pain":

1. *"Is your team not prospecting or are they not prospecting effectively?"* The sales team might actually be working very hard. The real problem may be the lack of specific sales skills: they don't know how to effectively ask for referrals. The solution isn't about making the team work harder, it's about helping them work smarter.

2. *"Do you have the right people on your team?"* No amount of sales training is going to help if you have a team of unmotivated salespeople. This prospect might have a hiring problem, not a prospecting problem. The better solution might be to help them install a more effective hiring and selection process.

3. *"What accountability and tracking systems do you have in place?"* If there isn't any measurement happening, it might be better for this prospect to invest in sales management training instead of prospecting training for the team. Lack of accountability is a leadership issue, not a sales issue.

You can improve your ability to learn your prospect's underlying problem. Apply the soft skill of problem solving. A systematic approach to asking effective questions helps you look at business challenges from all perspectives. Better questions produce better solutions.

Determine the Commitment to Change

It's not enough to learn about a client's pain. In order to save yourself valuable time, you also need to know how committed the client is to curing that pain. We teach our clients not to believe their prospects—nicely.

This doesn't mean your prospects are lying. It simply means that salespeople must get better at gathering evidence to see how serious their prospects are about making a change. We have seen more than one salesperson "buy the buying signal" and write up a proposal, only to have the prospect say, "We've put this on the back burner." That response happens because the salesperson didn't ask the tough questions during the meeting to really determine whether or not the prospect was serious about changing or improving.

Have you ever told a friend that you want to lose weight, eat better, and get more sleep? And are you still thinking about but not using that treadmill in the basement? Are you still buying potato chips, hoping that somehow they are part of one of the four major food groups? And are you continuing to watch late-night shows and waking up tired to an early-morning alarm?

So, were you lying to your friend when you shared your goals for better health? No, you simply stated a want without any indicator or evidence of commitment to change.

Your prospects aren't any different. Many share a want or desire and as a result, salespeople believe they have a qualified prospect. They get excited and don't ask further questions to determine the prospect's commitment level to achieving the want or eliminating the pain.

Again, psychologists understand this principle well. A good psychologist knows she cannot prescribe any solution to a problem until the patient shows a commitment to changing his behavior and actions. Let's look at an example of what happens when a doctor gets impatient, doesn't conduct a diagnostic meeting, and prescribes a solution too soon.

A patient sets up an appointment with the psychologist. The doctor asks, *"What brings you in today?"* The patient immediately launches into his problems. *"Well, doctor, I have an anger management issue. I came home yesterday and kicked my dog because I had a bad day at work. Then, I sat down and drank a quart of Jack Daniels while eating a giant bag of chips. I fell asleep on the couch and woke up with a terrible crick in my neck and had another lousy day at work."*

The psychologist is eager to share her expertise. This is not the first time she has heard these issues. *"Bob, let's deal with one problem at a time. First, here is the number of a good vet. He can help you get your dog taken care of. Next, let me give you the number of the local AA group. They meet at 9 a.m. every Monday and Wednesday. And you're in luck, because right after that meeting, Weight*

Watchers meets, so you can attend that right after the AA meeting. I think that should take care of your dog, binge drinking, and overeating. Any questions?"

Is Bob really going to make any long-term changes in his life? No, because the psychologist went into solution mode instead of asking questions. She didn't ask the tough questions to determine how committed this patient is to changing behaviors.

Now, returning to the sales world, let's say a prospect shares a problem with you, such as, *"We are having quality issues from our existing vendor. We need to make a change."* The effective salesperson manages her emotions and recognizes that the prospect simply made a statement, not a commitment to change. She doesn't believe, and—nicely—asks more questions to test whether or not she has a suspect or prospect.

"You've had a relationship with this vendor for ten years. Is this quality problem big enough to discontinue that relationship? How committed is the company to getting this issue fixed?" A good salesperson makes that prospect prove to her that there is a commitment to change prior to writing up any recommendations.

Get into the right mindset and don't believe—nicely. It helps you manage your emotions and ask good qualifying questions that uncover the prospect's commitment to change. As strange as it may sound, some prospects just like to meet with salespeople to vent and whine. Don't confuse complaints with commitment to invest and improve.

Agree and Align

Another reason salespeople don't ask enough questions during a sales meeting is because the prospect evokes a flight-or-flight response by stating an objection. The salesperson starts reacting and questioning shuts down and information spewing starts up. Here are a few examples that can trigger fight-or-flight responses in salespeople.

PROSPECT: *"I don't know if one company has all the answers."*

SALESPERSON: *"Well, our company has a deep bench of experts. We've been in business for over 50 years and blah, blah, blah."* (The salesperson is going into defend-and-justify mode and is "fighting" for the sale.)

PROSPECT: *"We're not sure the timing is right to move forward on this project."*

SALESPERSON: *"Okay, I'll give you a call back in a couple of weeks."* (The salesperson went into flight mode, putting the prospect in the pipeline for future follow-up. She didn't ask a key qualifying question, *"Is there ever going to be a good time?"*)

The astute salesperson recognizes the potential trigger and manages her emotions by applying a skill we call "agree and align." When a prospect states an objection, avoid the natural response, which is to push back. Instead, agree with the prospect and validate his position. When you agree and validate, there is nothing to trigger a fight-or-flight response.

Aligning and agreeing is a form of "pattern interrupt," another communication tool from the world of neurolinguistic programming. It's often used during sales meetings to disarm both you and the prospect's knee-jerk defense mechanisms and programmed responses. It's doing the opposite of what the prospect is expecting you to do. And it helps you change your response as well. Instead of slipping into fight-or-flight mode, you set the stage for further conversation and questions. Let's see how this skill changes the dynamics of a sales conversation:

PROSPECT: *"I don't know if one company has all the answers."*

AGREE: *"You know, I've got to agree with you. I don't know if our company has all the answers either. Let's talk about specific answers you're looking for. Then we should be able to see if our organization has the right solutions or not."*

PROSPECT: *"We're not sure the timing is right to move forward on this project."*

AGREE: *"It may not be the right time. Why don't we look further at the pros and cons of delaying the project? Then you and I can determine what's best for your organization."*

Empathy and self-awareness are important in executing this powerful selling skill. First, you must recognize when you are going into fight-or-flight mode. Then you need to put on the empathy hat and step into your prospect's shoes. When you put on the empathy hat, it is easy to agree with and validate the prospect's position—because of your sincere desire to know where their thoughts and perceptions are coming from.

New York Times columnist Thomas Friedman shared these words of wisdom with the graduating class of Williams College in Williamstown, Massachusetts:

> You can get away with really disagreeing with people as long as you show them the respect of really listening to what they have to say and taking into account when and if it makes sense. It's amazing how you can diffuse a whole roomful of angry people by just stating your answer to a question with the phrase, "You're making a legitimate point" or "I hear what you say" and really mean it. Never underestimate how much people just want to feel that they have been heard, and once you have given them that chance they will hear you.

There is no need to do combat with prospects and customers. Do the opposite of what they expect and validate their position. When people feel heard, they respond by lowering their defenses and engaging in conversation. It helps you ask more questions, learn their story, and discover what's really important to them.

Action Steps for Improving Your Questioning Skills

The inability to effectively ask questions and listen is probably the number one weakness of most sales professionals we work with. Due to these underdeveloped skills, salespeople often fail to uncover a prospect's true pain, and as a result they talk too much, write unqualified proposals, or get beat on price. There are four steps you can take to elevate your questioning skills and increase your income:

1. Evaluate how you set up your sales meetings.
2. Ask, don't tell.
3. Test the commitment to change.
4. Learn your prospect's story.

Step #1: Evaluate How You Set Up Your Sales Meetings

Review Chapter 5 and make sure you are setting up your sales meetings for a consultation, not a product dump. If you don't set clear expectations that you will be asking numerous questions in order to better understand the prospect's situation, none of what you learned in this chapter can be applied. There is a good chance that the prospect will push you into that not-so-nice place of prescribing before you have had a chance to fully diagnose his problem.

Step #2: Ask, Don't Tell

After each meeting, draw a circle and divide it into the time that you spent talking and the time the prospect talked. If you have a bigger piece of the pie, admit that you probably did more telling than asking, possibly boring the heck out of your prospects. And you didn't learn the prospect's story.

Analyze and determine what made you take over the meeting. What trigger caused your lips to start moving and your ears to quit listening:

> Did you lack patience and just want to get to the solution?
> Did you believe too quickly without gathering evidence for change?
> Did you go into fight-or-flight mode?

Once you figure out the trigger, put a strategy in place to stop the natural response to that trigger and correct your course. Ask yourself the 3Ws: Do I really know WHY this was a problem for this prospect? Do I know WHAT the current impact of the problem is for this prospect? Do I know WHAT the future impact is if the prospect doesn't get this problem fixed?

Manage your fight-or-flight reactions and realize that objections aren't a bad thing. In fact, it's better to have prospects who are willing to state concerns. It means they are trying to be open with you rather than hiding objections that you will never know about, and thus will never have a chance to thoroughly explore and discuss.

Step #3: Test the Commitment to Change

Good salespeople work only on the best-qualified opportunities. They are comfortable asking the prospect about their commitment level to solving an issue or challenge. Without such commitment, there isn't a reason to move forward in the sales process.

Ask this qualifying question during your meeting: *"Mr. Prospect, all companies have a lot of competing priorities. Where is getting this problem solved on your priority list, on a scale of one to ten?"* If the prospect responds with a five, it might be time to stop the engagement because the problem might be a nice-to-solve issue rather than a need-to-solve issue. Business is a two-way street. You have the right to work only with prospects that are serious about changing and improving.

Step #4: Learn Your Prospect's Story

Think how important it makes you feel when people want to learn more about you and your goals. Your prospects are just like you. Set up your next sales meeting with the sole intent of learning your prospect's story. When you sit down with a prospect, pretend you are charged with writing her autobiography. Gather facts, data, and personal stories. Don't be in a hurry to write the last chapter.

Former President Calvin Coolidge sums up this chapter nicely: "No man ever listened himself out of a job."

CHAPTER 7

Reaching Decision Makers

How to Better Connect and Meet

DO YOU LIVE in the city, the suburbs, or the country? Whatever your choice, many considerations most likely influenced your decision. Maybe you wanted a good school system for your kids. Perhaps you wanted to live in a neighborhood with big backyards, summer barbecues, and block parties. Or possibly the most important factor was having a property with plenty of room for your dogs to roam free. Whatever the consideration, there's a good chance that your next-door neighbor's reason for choosing this location was entirely different than yours.

This same decision-making process happens in business every day. Different people are involved in buying your product or service and each one has a different set of criteria for making a purchase. People and businesses buy for their own reasons, not yours. This is a basic principle to remember when trying to navigate through a company's decision-making process.

Salespeople study the prospect company's organizational charts and identify various buying influences in the organization. There is a heavy emphasis placed on meeting all the buyers in order to win business. Salespeople consider selling strategies and approaches to gaining entry and penetration into the account and fill out long pre-call planning forms that put prospects in nice little boxes. Prospects are assigned names such as the economic buyer (the person who writes the check), the user buyer (the person using your product or executing your service), and the power buyer (the big boss).

So with all this research and pre-call planning, why do so many salespeople still end up in dead-end sales scenarios where they are stuck meeting with non–decision makers? Or if they are successful at setting up meetings with the right buyers, why do they lose to a competitor who didn't have as good a solution?

There are a few reasons. Most pre-call strategy meetings neglect soft skills in their analysis of the opportunity. For example, what is the personality and mindset of the various people in the organizational charts? How do these individuals personally make decisions? What do you need to do or say in order to better relate to each of them?

You can make assumptions based on their position: the CFO, often called the economic buyer, is going to be looking at the return on investment. The CEO, typically the power buyer, will be focused on services that help with growth and acquisitions. But it's important for a salesperson to look beyond the title.

Some people make decisions in order to mitigate risks. Others thrive on making decisions that involve risks and trying something new. Some people make decisions quickly, others need time to process and analyze. Prospects can have the same title of CEO, and yet each person makes decisions differently. One more review of the organizational chart is not going to win business if you don't know how to read and connect with the different types of buyers.

Another area that is often missed in pre-call planning is the discussion about the importance of assertiveness in getting meetings set with all the buying influences. You *know* you are supposed to set up meetings with various potential buyers. So why aren't you doing it?

No amount of pre-call planning is going to help close business if you aren't able to ask for what you need in order to conduct business. It's a classic case of working on the wrong end of the problem.

Let's take a look at the soft skills needed to uncover your prospect's personal and corporate decision-making criteria. You'll recognize these emotional intelligence skills from earlier chapters: self-awareness, interpersonal skills, assertiveness, self-regard, and delayed gratification. They are all critical in helping you connect and meet with all the buying influences.

How People Make Decisions

Sales training programs usually focus heavily on identifying the buying influences in the prospect's organizational chart. Facilitators rarely discuss the people behind the labels and titles, each of whom has their own way of processing information and making decisions. It's one thing to identify a buying influence, it's another to know how to engage and connect in order to learn what's driving their decisions.

Interpersonal skills are essential at this selling stage. Good salespeople have the ability to connect and build relationships with a variety of people, not just people like themselves. And when you are selling to larger accounts, there will always be a variety of buyers to meet, relate to, and influence.

In order to better understand who is sitting in these decision-making chairs, we teach the DISC communication model, which helps you understand how your buyers communicate and make decisions based on their own personal style. If you are not aware of who you are dealing with, there is a good chance that the prospect is not going to connect with you because of your inability to read the prospect and adapt your sales approach.

One of our goals in teaching this communication model is to raise your awareness of how you react to certain communication styles. The more you know about who you are meeting with, the less likely you are to respond with nonproductive selling behaviors.

Dr. William Moulton Marston is given credit for this communication model. His book, *Emotions of Normal People* (Routledge, 1999; Cooper Press, 2007), provides descriptive words that outline a person's observable behavior and the characteristics that accompany that behavior. For example, some buyers thrive on receiving a lot of detail and data when meeting with a salesperson. Other buyers' eyes glaze over at the thought of looking at charts, graphs, and data. The emotionally intelligent salesperson is always looking for clues about how the prospect likes to interact and make decisions.

Dr. Marston's research categorizes people into four areas, based on specific characteristics commonly referred to as "personality types." These four types are typically known as:

Driver or Dominant

Influencer or Influence

Steady Relator or Steadiness

Cautious Thinker or Conscientious

Successful salespeople include this people analysis in their pre-call preparation. This additional knowledge of their prospect helps them understand the what, why, and how behind each person's decision-making process.

The Driver

Characteristics. The Driver doesn't need or want to invest a lot of time in small talk when meeting with a salesperson for the first time. He will spend not more than two to three minutes in light conversation, then shift his body position, take charge of the meeting, and get down to business.

Here's the problem. Salespeople have been taught to conduct

small talk in order to build rapport. What they have not been taught is that some buyers don't appreciate small talk at the beginning of an appointment. Excessive talking doesn't appeal to this hard-charging buyer and the meeting is over before it even starts.

The Driver is aggressive, competitive, and likes to win. He is direct and bottom-line oriented. The Driver is open to new ideas because it may help him win and take his department or company to the next level of success. This buyer is not worried about the details and makes decisions quickly. He is interested in getting from A to Z without covering the entire alphabet.

How to Communicate and Sell to This Personality Type. Stop talking and get down to business. This prospect will talk about personal subjects, but only after business has been addressed. Be prepared to be challenged by this prospect because this personality type is looking for results and doesn't like to waste time.

Many Drivers intimidate salespeople because of their direct, sometimes abrupt style. This is where the soft skill of self-awareness comes into play. Recognize that their direct communication style can send you into fight-or-flight mode. You might start getting defensive with this prospect and try to talk over him. Or you rush through your sales process and don't ask enough questions because you just want to get out of the meeting. Because you got flustered, you miss uncovering key information that would help you craft a better solution. You might lose business to a competitor who didn't react, asked the right questions, and as a result presented a better recommendation.

Manage your emotional response and recognize that bottom-line conversation is just the way this person communicates. It's not personal.

A few years ago, I was meeting with a prospect for the first time. Dan is a successful, no-nonsense business owner. Right in the middle of our conversation, Dan threw a curve ball into the conversation and asked me a direct question: "Are you any good?" That question might have been perceived as intimidating. However, I knew I was in front of a Driver and didn't react. I paused and answered, "Yes, I am very good." That was the end of that question and the conversation continued. We wound up doing business together and our meetings were always direct and to the point.

Good salespeople prepare questions that align with the Driver's communication style and decision-making criteria, such as:

▶ What specific outcomes are you looking for in this project?

▶ How will this position your department/company in the marketplace?

▶ Who is your biggest competitor and what are they doing right?

▶ What are your growth plans? Are you on track or behind?

▶ Who and what is your biggest obstacle to growth?

▶ At the end of the day, what are three things you want to make sure get accomplished?

Note that all of the questions are geared toward results, and taking things to a next level.

The Influencer

Characteristics. The Influencer is more commonly known as an extrovert. She likes to talk, tell jokes, and is generally trusting and optimistic. The Influencer is motivated by recognition and status. She likes new ideas and products and makes decisions quickly and impulsively, often without thinking through the downside of the purchase.

How to Communicate and Sell to This Personality Type. Sales trainers like to ask this question: "What happens when an Influencer salesperson gets together with an Influencer prospect?" The answer—nothing, because the entire meeting was about having fun. Salespeople often get caught up in this buyer's enthusiasm and forget the reason for the appointment: something called business. Increase your emotional self-awareness and manage your emotions. Make sure that you are building both rapport and a business case when meeting with an Influencer.

The Driver salesperson often alienates the Influencer because he forgets the importance of small talk to this buyer, which is the opposite of his style. He gets down to business too quickly, which decreases the likeability factor. Pay attention and use your empathy skills to better read your prospect and adapt your approach. Know when to chat and when to conduct business.

It's important to be cognizant of this buyer's impulsive decision-making style. This prospect, more than any of the others, needs to be asked questions that help her look at the downside of the purchase as well as the upside in order to prevent buyer's remorse.

You may be puzzled when this prospect decides not to move forward because she seemed really excited about the product in the initial stages of the selling process. And because of the buyer's enthusiasm, you start believing you have a deal. You get sloppy in your qualification process and don't ask all the right questions, the tough questions.

This buyer really was ready to buy until she spoke to a colleague who asked tough questions that begin with, "What about . . . ," "Did you consider. . . ," and "What happens when . . . ?" All are questions that *you* should have asked during the meeting. Now the prospect starts having second thoughts and additional questions—none of which you are present to respond to—and the sale gets derailed.

When meeting with this buyer, you need to manage your emotions, especially your optimism, and not get carried away by the prospect's enthusiasm.

Good questions to prepare for this buyer are:

- ▶ How will this decision improve your position/department in the company?
- ▶ What can we do to help you look better?
- ▶ Let's look at the downside of this. What are some of the challenges or concerns in moving forward?
- ▶ Is there really any substantial impact to the organization if you don't address this issue?
- ▶ What are questions you will be asked regarding return on investment?

Focus on finding evidence for change or acquisition, not just on fun and providing information about your product or service. Ask tough questions during the sales meeting to prevent potential "buyer's remorse" before you've even sold anything!

The Steady Relator

Characteristics. The Steady Relator is a pleasant person who is described as amiable and easygoing. These buyers are relaxed and cordial. Often, they are the first person to ask you if you'd like water or coffee. (Drivers and Influencers don't even know you need water because they are too busy getting down to business or talking.)

Steady Relators are good team players. They are motivated by serving and helping people, both internal and external customers. It's important to note that they don't like change or confrontation. The Steady Relator is very loyal, which can be a double-edged sword. They are great customers because of their loyalty. They are also tough prospects because of their loyalty to the existing relationship. Their pace of buying is slower and more methodical than the Driver and Influencer.

How to Communicate and Sell to This Personality Type. First of all, slow down and build a relationship before talking about your product or service. Ask questions about their family or hobbies. Learn how they got started in the business and what they like best about their job. Get their views on how to best serve their team or their customers. Find out what good service looks like to them in order to align your solutions and recommendations with that viewpoint.

Be aware of their hesitation to be a trendsetter. More than one salesperson has blown a sales meeting with a Steady Relator by introducing their product as the "latest and newest thing on the market." Those might be magic words for the Driver and Influencer; they are not magic words for the Steady Relator.

It's important to address existing relationships with this type of buyer because of their strong sense of loyalty. Salespeople like to skip over this potential objection for fear of losing the sale. But good salespeople show empathy and validate the importance of relationships. Knowing that Steady Relators avoid conflict, it's important for you to bring up this potential objection because this prospect is not going to put it on the agenda. This loyal buyer sometimes sticks with below-average service in order to avoid the conflict or perceived hassle of change.

Good questions to ask this buyer are:

► How do you see this product helping your internal/external clients?

► What does good service look like to you?

► What makes good service so important to you?

► What don't you like about our products or services? (You might preface the comment with, "We understand that no one is perfect," giving them an easy way to confront you about this.)

► Let's talk about your existing vendor. Relationships are important. Can you share with me your biggest concern in switching?

Because they are amiable and nonconfrontational, it's easy to confuse a pleasant meeting with a Steady Relator, with a qualified opportunity. Use your empathy skills to see if there are any non-verbal clues being given by this prospect as to whether or not they are really comfortable with you and your offering. Don't confuse their hospitality with commitment to change or buy.

The Cautious Thinker

Characteristics. The last type of prospect, the Cautious Thinker, is commonly known as the "analytical buyer." This buyer can often throw salespeople off their game because they may come across a little aloof. The Cautious Thinker likes data and more data. This need for data has caused more than one sales meeting to end poorly because the salesperson didn't come prepared to deliver facts and figures. Some salespeople try to fake it by stating a general statistic, only to get caught when the Cautious Thinker asks, "And where did you get that number?"

This buyer is a good critical thinker, so she asks hard questions during a sales meeting. She makes decisions on data, not "fluff and stuff." This is the buyer who reads manuals and knows how to program everything on his phone and television. If you are a Driver or an Influencer, you may have difficulty selling to a Cautious Thinker because of your own lack of need or desire for detail. Be alert to this; prepare, prepare, prepare for this prospect.

How to Communicate and Sell to This Personality Type. This buyer will ask a lot of questions to determine your credibility and your company's credibility. They want to know how long you've been in the business and who some of your customers are. Some untrained salespeople take offense at these questions, thinking the prospect doubts their capability to deliver. Such questions send salespeople into fight mode or flight mode, causing them to get nervous. The meeting turns into a product dump meeting or the salesperson shuts down, not able to think of one good question by which to redirect the conversation back to needs and wants.

Asking a lot of questions is simply how the Cautious Thinker processes information and makes decisions. They need context before they feel comfortable going into a sales conversation.

This buyer also likes guarantees and warranties. One of his main criteria, when making a purchase, is to mitigate risk. Cautious Thinkers also like quality, so don't be quick to concede your price, even when they start negotiating. They value quality over price any day of the week.

Good questions to ask this buyer are:

- ▶ What specific criteria are you looking for in making this decision?

- ▶ What information can I provide about our company or my background?

- ▶ In the past when you have purchased _____, what were your top five criteria? What made those five qualities rise to the top of your selection process?

- ▶ How much will quality play in your decision? How do you define quality?

- ▶ What guarantees are you looking for?

What is your biggest concern about moving forward?

These buyers make decisions very slowly because of their high need for data, making right decisions, and perfection. They suffer from "analysis paralysis," often requesting more and more information to ensure a good decision is being made.

Working with this type of buyer requires delayed gratification skills. It's not going to be a quick sale, so you must be willing to put in the work before you are awarded the business.

Salespeople who need instant gratification get frustrated selling to this type of buyer because of the buyer's decision-making style. They might quit calling on this buyer because of his longer decision-making process or start pushing for a decision too soon in the sales process. They lose business to a salesperson possessing delayed-gratification skills, who understands this buyer and knows the sales process will take longer and is willing to put in the work to collect the reward of a sale.

Case Study

One of our clients in the financial planning industry expressed frustration over three prospects who had expressed a desire to move their portfolios over to her company due to the average service and returns they were receiving from their existing financial planners. Despite their dissatisfaction, all three were dragging their feet in making the final decision.

After attending our workshop and learning about the DISC communication model, she identified all three prospects as most likely Steady Relators. They were very nice people, valued relationships, and didn't like conflict or change. We coached her to call each prospect and validate the importance of relationships and loyalty. We also coached her to avoid putting the prospects in a position of perceived conflict and offered to call their existing financial planners, thank them for their years of service, and explain that the clients were ready to move onto a different company to handle their financial needs.

Our client showed up to the next workshop with a big smile on her face. Two of the three prospects took her up on the offer and moved their book of business. Our client gained two new customers because she understood how they made decisions. She used her empathy skills to validate their feelings and also put the burden of delivering the bad news of change on her own shoulders, rather than the prospects'.

Your interpersonal skills are important because you sell to a wide variety of buyers. It would be easier if we could sell to people just like ourselves because there would be no need to adapt or change our approach. The most successful salespeople we know are able to build relationships with a variety of personality styles.

Are You Meeting with Mr. No?

Now that you know what personality type is sitting in the chair, it's time to make sure you get meetings with all the people influencing the buying decision. One of the biggest complaints we hear from salespeople during the decision stage of the sales process is that they are stuck with a non–decision maker and/or can't get meetings with other buying influences.

Salespeople who end up in these dead-end situations usually spend their time analyzing what selling skills they are lacking. While there might be hard skills missing, we find that lack of emotional intelligence skills such as self-regard, self-actualization, and assertiveness are equal contributors to these challenges.

Salespeople know, either through the school of hard knocks or through training delivered by the owner or sales manager, that they need to get in front of the "right" decision maker, usually someone in the C-suite. This can be the chief financial officer, chief marketing officer, or chief operating officer. Salespeople know who they are supposed to call on to make the sale, so what's the real reason salespeople still call too low in the organizational chart?

We have found that many salespeople are intimidated by the C-suite buyer. This isn't a selling skill issue; this is a lack-of-confidence issue. Lack of confidence prevents them from setting and managing expectations to meet with these buyers.

Salespeople seem to think that this buyer wakes up every day with the goal of stumping salespeople. Their self-talk or internal belief system says, "I'm not worthy. This person has a bigger title than me. They are going to ask me a question and I won't have the answer."

We have some good news for you. This buyer is too busy to put together a game plan for stumping you. The C-level buyer is willing to engage with a salesperson who makes her life easier. Ask yourself this important question: What are you doing everyday to make yourself more valuable to this buyer?

Jill Konrath, author of *SNAP Selling* (Portfolio Hardcover, 2010), talks about today's crazy busy buyers. She notes that while these busy executives will meet with salespeople, they don't have time to waste. She warns salespeople to stop making "I'm just checking in" calls and start making "let me add value to your day" calls.

For example, do you understand how to read a profit-and-loss statement? If not, how can you have a quality conversation and add value when dealing with a prospect charged with running a profit center? How can you uncover potential problems or make suggestions if you don't understand the basics of running a business or a department? Are you reading trade publications? Business books? If not, how will you make a meaningful contribution to the conversation? What insights will you provide that your prospect hasn't had time to learn or read about?

This is where the emotional intelligence skill of self-actualization shows up. The lifelong learning salesperson takes time to learn and understand things that make them of more value to every decision maker they work with. This salesperson asks himself this question every month: am I smarter than I was thirty days ago? What did I learn this month that will add value to every interaction with clients and prospects?

A top real estate broker in Denver makes it a habit to call all her prospects monthly. The phone call isn't to sell, but to share a specific piece of information that adds value to their business. As a result, her prospects looked forward to taking her phone calls. And when their lease is up for renewal, she has already established how much value she can add to their lives. It's not a hard decision for prospects to move their brokerage business to her.

There is an easy way to grow your confidence. Go into every

meeting prepared to add value, value, and more value. A funny thing called a "sale" generally happens after that.

Are You Asking the Right Question?

You are practically guaranteed *not* to get meetings with all the decision makers if you ask the following outdated sales question: "Who besides yourself is involved in this decision?" It's a dead-end question because 50 percent of the time the prospect replies, *"It's me. I make the decision when it comes to this purchase. Why don't you go ahead and put together a proposal."*

You know full well that this person hasn't made a final decision on anything in the last twenty years. Now you're in that difficult place of trying to get other meetings set up without offending his contact because he asked a dumb question. You know who you need to meet with based on your past experiences of winning and losing deals. So why are you asking the question?

We suggest that you eliminate the question and simply state what you need in order to make an effective recommendation. It's fairly simple. You will need to speak to all the people being impacted by this decision, otherwise you are guessing at the proper solution. And guessing isn't a good use of anyone's time or money.

For example, you might say:

> "Joan, you and I have had a good meeting today and I appreciate that. I think there are some things my company can do to help you solve some of your challenges with document management. However, before I can comfortably put together a proposal, I will also need to speak with your Director of IT and your CFO.
>
> One of the reasons we have a good reputation is that we take time to meet with all parties affected by this purchase. We work hard to learn what's important to them and as result are able to make an effective recommendation that includes everyone's input. Without

those conversations, we are just guessing at the right solution. Can you help me get those meetings set up?"

The above statement is truth telling at best. Truth telling requires the emotional intelligence skills of assertiveness and self-regard and the successful salesperson has both. She is confident and assertive enough to state what she needs in order for this opportunity to be an effective use of her time.

Deal with Potential Problems Upfront

Apply a lesson from Chapter 5 and deal with potential problems that can occur when working with busy decision makers.

More than once, a salesperson has driven an hour across town, only to find out that the key decision maker had to fly out of town unexpectedly. However, the non–decision maker always seems to be able to make it to the meeting and promises to give any information you discuss that day to the big boss. After the meeting, the non–decision maker asks you to put together a proposal. You put a proposal together that lacks the key decision maker's needs and wants. The non–decision maker calls you back and says, "Thanks for your time. We are going another direction."

Meanwhile, your proactive, assertive competitor gets a meeting with the true decision maker. She builds a relationship, uncovers specific needs and wants, and delivers a "spot on" solution that wins the business.

Did you lose the business because you didn't have the solution? Or was it because you were not proactive and assertive enough to set expectations for how you do business? We suggest it's the latter. An assertive conversation that avoids this potential problem sounds like this:

"Pete, based on our conversation today, let's go ahead and set up another meeting. Since Jacob is the head of finance, we will need to have him in the meeting to make sure he understands the return on investment for this purchase. I know how busy Jacob's schedule is, so I will call a couple of days before our meeting to make sure the time still works for him. If it doesn't, we'll go ahead and reschedule for another day, since I can't put together an effective recommendation without his input."

The assertive salesperson is comfortable setting and managing expectations for a mutually successful meeting. He deals with the potential problem before it becomes a problem.

Action Steps for Improving Your Ability to Reach Decision Makers

As you can see, understanding how people and corporations make decisions is not a cookie-cutter process. We tell our clients that understanding this process is both textbook and real world. "Textbook" is what we refer to as the classic study of the company's organizational chart, identification of the buying influences and their roles and responsibilities. "Real world" is recognizing that that every person and company makes decisions differently and sometimes their decision-making process doesn't align with the textbook version.

For example, we see many companies that hang mission statements on the wall proudly stating, "We empower our people to make decisions." Then, when it comes time for the company to make a purchase, you quickly learn that all empowerment goes out the window. You discover there is only one true buyer at the company and that buyer is in the corner office—the power buyer. (This is the same buyer that had the empowerment posters made.)

The organizational charts show titles and reporting relationships, but remember that the chart is filled with people who make decisions their own way, and make them for their own reasons. Here are three steps that will improve your ability to navigate through the decision step of the sales process:

1. Review the way you interact with different personality types.

2. Have another truth-telling conversation with yourself.

3. Ask yourself how good you are at making decisions.

Improve your skills in this important stage and you will be one step closer to improving your close ratios.

Step #1: Review the Way You Interact with Different Personality Types

Does the Driver make you nervous and start you down the road of pitching and selling versus consulting and listening? Does the Influencer turn your sales meeting into a social event rather than a business conversation? Do you get so comfortable with the Steady Relator that you neglect to ask enough questions during the meeting, mistaking her hospitality for interest? Did you show up to the meeting with the Cautious Thinker prepared with answers and data in order to connect with his buying criteria?

Listen and look for clues to determine what type of buyer you have in front of you so you can adjust and adapt. The Driver will use words like "at the end of the day" and "next level." The Influencer will be doing most of the talking. The Steady Relator will have pictures of his family or his team on the walls of his office. His demeanor is relaxed and calm. The Cautious Thinker will have a very neat desk and office. He might come across as aloof or cold.

Track your wins and losses to see if they are connected to the prospect's behavioral style. Analyze each loss and ask yourself what you could have done to better connect with this prospect. What questions could you or should you have prepared to uncover their personal buying criteria?

We had a salesperson ask us, "Is it okay to just call on people like myself? That seems like it would be easier." Our answer was,

"Yes, but only if you can afford to leave behind 50 percent of your opportunities."

Learn how to read your prospects and adapt your approach and style. You will be able to sell to any behavioral style, not just prospects who are similar to your personality.

Step #2: Have Another Truth-Telling Conversation with Yourself

What is the reason you are not scheduling meetings with the right decision maker or all the decision makers? Is your self-talk getting the best of you, convincing you that the C-suite buyer is a tougher buyer or you have nothing of value to share? Are you spending so much time worrying about your ability to perform well that you don't even try to schedule an appointment with this buyer?

Set up a meeting with one of your executive clients. Ask your client for his opinion on what he wants and expects from salespeople. You might be surprised at how simple the answer is: competency, integrity, and responsiveness. All of those qualities are within your control.

If you're not sure of how to have a financial conversation with a high-level executive, maybe you aren't adding value to the conversation. Ask the CFO or someone in your accounting department to give you a Finance 101 class to understand the business of business. Take a class at the local college and develop your business acumen. Start subscribing to industry publications. Read business books and learn how great business leaders think and act. Adding value to a sales conversation is in your full control.

Check your assertiveness. Are you asking for what you need or just accepting what you get? You know what it takes to put together an effective recommendation. Ask for what you need or get used to writing practice proposals that are missing input from key decision makers.

Step #3: Ask Yourself How Good You Are at Making Decisions

If you aren't very good at making decisions, how effective are you going to be at asking your prospects and customers to make decisions? Salespeople that are wishy-washy in making decisions in their personal and professional lives tend to expect and get the same behavior from their prospects.

One of the things we've noticed with good salespeople is that they don't waste a lot of time worrying about "what happens if I make the wrong decision?" They know that even wrong decisions can be good because they learn that powerful thing called a lesson. The new knowledge from the lesson helps them do better on the next opportunity.

Decision makers make decisions. If you want to shorten your sales cycle and increase your wins, get good at scheduling meetings with these individuals. Do your pre-call planning and analysis but never forget that you are meeting with people. Learn what makes people tick. Adapt your approach so you connect and build relationships with a variety of buyers.

CHAPTER 8

Checkbook

Get Paid What You Are Worth

YOU MIGHT RECALL the funny scene in the movie *Jerry McGuire* where sports agent Jerry McGuire and his potential client Rod Tidwell are on the phone, yelling back and forth as Rod questions his agent's resolve to represent him successfully. It all culminates in the famous line, "Show me the money!"

If salespeople would apply this mantra as part of their selling strategy, they would make a lot more money and save countless hours pursuing unqualified opportunities. *"Show me the money, Mr. Prospect. Are you willing and able to invest in my product or service before I spend my time writing up a proposal?"*

Many salespeople are weak in this stage of the sales process that we call "checkbook." They fail to ask enough qualifying questions to determine whether their solution fits the prospect's budget—their checkbook. They learn too late that the prospect is buying only on price, not value. They discount too quickly when faced with a good negotiator, or they write a proposal for a prospect who is really just doing research to make sure his existing vendor is still offering him a good price and value.

Here are a couple of common scenarios we hear from frustrated salespeople who are not getting paid what they are worth. In the first, the salesperson does her best to discuss the prospect's budget, only to hear that the prospect has no idea how much money has been committed to the project. "Just put some numbers together for a review," he tells her. The dutiful salesperson puts in hours of time writing a proposal, often involving personnel from other departments. The salesperson then meets with the prospect to go over the proposal. The prospect flips to the back page, looks at the investment required, and says, "That's too high . . . more than I wanted to spend." Since the salesperson has spent so much time on the proposal, she doesn't want to lose the deal, so she quickly lowers her price without applying any selling skills such as countering with a concession strategy or simply asking more questions. As a result, she wins the business on thin margins, resulting in a very thin commission check.

In the second scenario, the prospect asks the salesperson to redo the entire proposal because the investment is too high. The salesperson still doesn't know the budget and invests even more time writing up a new recommendation. He presents the new and improved proposal to the prospect only to hear, "We are going to put this on the back burner. It's just not in the budget this year."

It's tempting for the salesperson to take the easy way out and blame the company's pricing structure: "If our company had better pricing, I could close some business." Salespeople also blame their prospects: "In today's economy, no one buys on value . . . only on low price." It's easy to poke holes in these excuses by asking the following questions:

▶ If no one is buying on price, why is your higher-price competitor still in business?

➤ If your prospects are only interested in a low price, why are they setting an appointment with you knowing you are positioned in the market as the high-price, high-value solution?

The reality is that it's not about the company pricing model or the prospect. It's about lack of soft and hard skills. When we cover the checkbook segment of the sales process during sales training, we ask our participants two questions:

1. When would you *like* to find out whether your prospect is willing and able to invest in your service: before you write a proposal or after you write a proposal?" (*One hundred percent of the participants raise their hands and reply, "Before."*)

2. When *do* you find out that your prospect is willing and able to invest in your products or services: before you write a proposal or after you write a proposal?" (*The response dramatically changes as half the participants raise their hands and reply, "After."*)

It is the knowing-and-doing gap showing up again. Salespeople know what they *should* do. They know they should discuss and agree on the investment for their product or services before writing up any type of recommendation. But way too many still waste their time writing practice proposals that end up sitting on someone's desk or in the wastebasket.

The frustrated owner or sales manager does her best to correct the price-shopping and practice-proposal problem. She reinforces the value of their product or service to the team one more time. Money is invested in negotiation skills training. She explains the importance of uncovering the prospect's budget before writing up a recommendation. In some companies, compensation plans are changed in hopes of getting the salesperson to sell at full margin. Yet many of these well-intended strategies don't work as well as desired because they don't get to the root of why salespeople don't charge or get paid what they are worth.

Certain sales and negotiation skills are absolutely helpful when trying to uncover and validate the prospect's budget. However, these hard selling skills will only be executed if you are able to manage your emotions and apply equally important soft skills.

Our observation of salespeople who are exceptionally good at closing business at full margin indicates that they possess many similar emotional intelligence qualities: self-awareness, assertiveness, self-confidence. They are self-aware and recognize certain triggers from prospects and customers that tempt them to discount. Assertiveness shows up again in this selling stage. Good salespeople are comfortable asking for what they need. And they know they need to get the prospect's budget before they invest time in writing a proposal. Self-confident salespeople know they bring high value and outcomes to their customers, and that conviction helps them stand their ground during tough negotiations.

Let's explore each of these competencies and a few more to see their correlation in helping you uncover your prospect's budget and get paid what you are worth. Our discussion will help you better qualify opportunities, decrease writer's cramp caused by practice proposals, and increase your commissions.

What Is Your "Money Talk"?

In order to become comfortable discussing budgets with your prospects, it's important to understand your relationship to money because it plays a big role in effectively executing the checkbook stage of the selling process.

During training, we take participants down memory lane with an exercise where they discuss with peers how money was viewed in their childhood homes. We ask them to discuss what message they received from their parents regarding money. Here are the common statements we hear:

- ▶ "It's not polite to talk about money."
- ▶ "Money doesn't grow on trees."
- ▶ "Money is the root of all evil."
- ▶ "Don't buy something unless it's on sale."
- ▶ "Do you think I'm made of money?"
- ▶ "Money can't buy you happiness."

If you take a look at these messages, none are very useful in helping a salesperson feel comfortable talking about money and charging for value. Statements such as "Money is the root of all evil" actually imply that if you are getting paid what you are worth, perhaps you are taking advantage of your prospect or customer.

A key emotional intelligence skill used during the checkbook stage is self-awareness. You must recognize triggers that cause you to concede to prices or terms that are not a true win-win for you or your company.

Consider the statement, "It's not polite to talk about money" and the possible emotional triggers it can elicit. A client shares this story from her childhood. Chantal recalled a favorite uncle who had just purchased a new car and was showing it off to her mother and father. She didn't know talking about money was considered bad manners so she piped up and asked, "How much did it cost?" Both parents quickly admonished her for asking the question. Her lesson learned at an early age was that money was none of her business.

After taking part in our exercise, Chantal became aware of the real reason she wasn't discussing money with her prospects and customers. Unknowingly, she was taking Mom, Dad, and Uncle to her appointments.

When she heard prospects say something like, "I am not comfortable sharing my budget with you," Chantal immediately went into flight mode and asked no further questions. She was a polite *and* unprofitable salesperson because she wasted a lot of time pursuing unqualified prospects who couldn't afford her services.

Once Chantal became aware of the trigger, she recognized how an old, outdated belief system concerning money was affecting her sales meetings. She was able to change her response and become more assertive. She initiated better money conversations with prospects, which uncovered their budgets and resulted in solutions better aligned with their checkbooks.

Selling skills were not holding Chantal back from getting paid what she was worth; soft skills were.

Other clients share stories of how money was a point of contention in their homes. One parent was a spender, for example, and another a saver. The lesson our clients learned at an early age was to avoid the discussion of money because it creates arguments and hard feelings. These salespeople avoid the money conversation because of this association. They cross their fingers and hope the prospect has money to invest while wasting time pursuing unqualified opportunities. And as we all know, hope is not a good selling strategy.

Change Your Response and Change Your Results

As we have mentioned, emotional intelligence skills can be learned. You are not destined to live with old thinking-and-doing patterns.

Self-aware salespeople understand possible triggers from the past and choose a different response. When the prospect says they don't know the budget or are hesitant to share it, the salesperson uses their empathy, assertiveness, and reality-testing skills to qualify the opportunity. They ask further questions to ensure they are not getting set up to write another practice proposal. Is the prospect willing and able to do business?

> "Mr. Prospect, most of our clients don't have a budget. That's not unusual. *(Empathy.)* However, other clients with similar challenges

> have invested between X and Y in order to eliminate the problem. Is that a range you are comfortable with?" (*Assertiveness and reality testing.*)

The salesperson is comfortable asking for a range and most prospects have a range in mind, even if the purchase is not a line item on the profit-and loss-statement.

> "Mr. Prospect, I'm curious about your hesitation to tell us your budget. Is it because you think we are going to come up with a magical number that just happens to use up your whole budget without giving you lower-priced options? (*Empathy. The prospect might have had a bad experience with a salesperson taking advantage of him.*) Or is it something else? If you are not comfortable giving us this information, we might have a problem. When we work with clients, we see it as a partnership. And at the foundation of that partnership is trust that we are not going to abuse your openness and honesty. What do you suggest we do?" (*Assertiveness and reality testing.*)

Emotional intelligence is about common sense. And common sense tells you that your prospects always have some type of budget; otherwise, how can they tell you that your prices are too high?

Examine your relationship with money. If you aren't comfortable talking about it, then you'll need to get comfortable wasting time and energy on unqualified opportunities.

What's your money talk?

Learn to Deal with Good Negotiators

Strong negotiators are skilled at using tactics designed to create emotional reactions. Jeanette Nyden, author of *Negotiation Rules* (Sales Gravy Press, 2009), addresses the importance of emotion management in negotiations. "It is imperative that you recognize tactics so you are not drawn into reactionary conversations," she writes. "If you hold the line, and calmly pack your bag, the prospect's tactic is not effective. If you get weak in the knees, and give in, it is effective. Ultimately, it is your choice to respond."

What great advice! Years ago, one of my clients successfully used a negotiating tactic with me. We were just getting ready to finalize a sizable project when he did the "throw-in-one-more-thing" tactic. He said, "This all looks good. By the way, we are having a retreat for our senior executives up at the Ritz Carlton in Beaver Creek, Colorado. It's on the weekend so we invite you to bring your husband. Could you throw in a morning of training that weekend?"

The idea of a weekend in the mountains with my husband at beautiful Beaver Creek Resort was enticing. I got excited and let my emotions get the best of me. I quickly said "yes" without any concession strategy such as, "How about if I throw in the morning training at half my fee?" Was it lack of selling skills or emotion management skills that led me to reply "yes" too quickly? It was absolutely a lack of soft skills, impulse control being one, that prevented me from using my hard skills of negotiation.

It's important to learn negotiation tactics and selling skills to recognize when they are being used during a meeting. I would never have spotted the tactic, however late, had I not invested in negotiation skills training for myself. When another prospect attempted a similar tactic that caused the excitement response, I recognized it. This time I did a much better job of managing my emotions and applied an effective counteroffer.

Case Study

A colleague shared a story that is a good example of a salesperson refusing to be influenced by prospects who use emotional triggers during negotiation. In this case, her soft skills yielded hard sales results.

Beverly is a consultant and presentation skills trainer. She had met with her prospect twice, interviewed all the buying influences, and had discussed budget. Deal flow was progressing nicely and they were ready to sign the contract.

As she and the prospect were outlining the final rollout of the training, her prospect leaned back in his chair and said, "Okay, let's discuss your fees." Beverly was a little puzzled, as they had already discussed her training fees. The prospect informed Beverly that he never paid full price for anything. He then asked her what she could do about her pricing. The prospect was using a negotiation tactic. Lower your price, he implied, or we may not have a deal.

Beverly did not have formal negotiation or sales training under her belt. What she did have was high self-regard and assertiveness. Beverly wasn't arrogant, but she knew the value she brought to her clients. She simply stated her position, the truth.

"Dan, I can't discount because I work with too many clients in this area and all of them are very comfortable paying this invest- ment due to the return they get from my training. I am not sure what to do since I can't lower my price. It wouldn't be fair to all of the other companies that I have worked with that have paid that investment. And the reality is, my calendar is really booked. It doesn't make sense to discount."

Dan was more than a little surprised at Beverly's unflinching commitment to her price. In the end, he hired Beverly and told her that she was the first "vendor" he'd ever paid at full fee.

Beverly managed her emotions and earned a new client without eroding her margins. Her confidence in her value helped Beverly stand her ground and not cave to price concessions. Soft skills earned this contract at full fee, not selling skills.

She also unknowingly applied a powerful negotiation skill, explained next.

Are You Willing to Walk?

Years ago, I attended my first negotiation skills training class. The instructor was a confident woman who walked across the room, put one foot up on the table, and opened the workshop with these words, "If you can't walk, you can't talk." She went on to explain the importance of not being attached to the outcome of a negotiation, referring to the power of being willing to walk away. This is an example of mindset over process. If you don't have the right mindset, and manage your emotions, you will not get paid what you're worth.

Walking away is not just a tactic made up by negotiation skills trainers. It's based on research that shows people want what they can't or don't have. In sales, the skill is often referred to as the "takeaway." Take the offer off the table and people seem to want it more than ever.

Retailers have used this concept for years. "Receive 50 percent off today!" "Only four more left!" Think of Black Friday and Cyber Monday. What is really driving people to get up at the strangest hours of the morning? Are the deals really that good or is it the concept of scarcity and the fear they might miss out on a good deal?

Most salespeople are hesitant to use this powerful approach. This puzzled us for years, and we kept throwing the wrong solutions at the problem in order to gain more buy-in to this selling concept. We'd share success stories and specific examples of how and when to use this tactic. Clients would practice and role-play in order to get comfortable with the idea of the "takeaway" or "walk away." Despite all this, we didn't see an increase in application of the method.

Once we gained an understanding of emotional intelligence, however, we discovered the root cause for lack of buy-in: poor emotion management. Salespeople lack self-awareness of how they respond to negotiation tactics used by prospects during a sales situation. When a prospect starts to negotiate, many salespeople go into fight-or-flight mode. They try to save the deal by discounting rather than showing a willingness to walk away.

Consider these common negotiation tactics used by prospects and the possible emotions they trigger—emotions that cause salespeople to discount without further questioning or counterstrategies.

> ► *"Your competitor is 20 percent lower. Can you match their price?"* (Panic, anger, desperation)

> ► *"We'd like to go with you. We think you have the best solution. However, your price is a little high."* (Flattery, panic, optimism)

> ► *"We've had a really tough year. Can you do any better?"* (Empathy and feeling sorry for the prospect)

It's important to note that these statements are tactics taught in formal negotiation skills training. They are designed to tap into a salesperson's head, his emotions, and get the salesperson to lower his price.

With self-awareness, you can have a "walk-away mindset," which allows you to remain calm and cool. Clarity of thought helps you redirect the conversation to one of value not price. Here are some examples of effective responses to such sales tactics:

PROSPECT: *"Your competition is 20 percent lower. Can you match their price?"*

SALESPERSON: *"I appreciate you being open about sharing their price. However, I am curious. Why are you still open to looking at us when you get the same value elsewhere at a lower price? As much as we'd like your business, if the competition can deliver the same value at the price you say, we can't blame you for going with them."*

The salesperson is managing his emotions and not reacting to the negotiation tactic. He is asking the prospect a very common-sense question. If the competitor is offering the exact same value at a lower price, what's the reason he is still in the game? Now, the prospect must justify the reason for wanting to continue the conversation with the salesperson.

PROSPECT: *"We'd like to go with you. We think you have the best solution. However, your price is a little high."*

SALESPERSON: *"Thank you. I appreciate your confidence in us. Let's review the proposal and figure out the highest return-on-investment areas. Then you and I can take a closer look at what we can remove from the proposal in order to hit your budget."*

Instead of reacting and quickly discounting, the salesperson asks the prospect to make a choice on what he wants to remove from the proposal. It's not about what can be discounted, it's about what the prospect is willing and able to commit to in order to solve a problem or take advantage of an opportunity.

PROSPECT: *"We've had a really tough year. Can you do any better?"*

SALESPERSON: *"I can understand. It's been a tough year for many of my customers. Would it make sense to further discuss if you should even be making this purchase? It might be better to delay this decision until next year."*

The salesperson is showing empathy, but also putting the responsibility of the purchase back on the prospect. She is comfortable walking away from the business, as it really might be the best thing to do for this prospect at this time.

There are many more responses and scenarios we could share that prove salespeople can execute strong selling skills when they improve their ability to manage emotions.

Examine Your Sales Pipeline

Another reason salespeople don't apply the powerful tactic of walking away relates to the beginning of the sales process: the sales pipeline.

Salespeople with empty sales pipelines have desperation breath. Prospects can spot this a mile away and leverage it to their financial advantage. Salespeople with empty sales pipelines have a hard time walking away from anything. Negotiation skills and tactics cannot be applied because their mindset is one of scarcity, not abundance.

When you have a full sales pipeline, you have a much greater chance of showing up to meetings with a wealthy mindset—a different attitude. Your thoughts change from "I need this deal" to "I can only take on serious prospects. I don't have time to write up practice proposals. And why in the world would I discount? I have too many other good opportunities to pursue."

Review the key concepts again in Chapter 3. Are you putting in the work of consistent prospecting to achieve the reward of a full sales pipeline? Do you have a defined sales activity plan that ensures consistent leads and qualified appointments?

When you have a full pipeline you are willing to walk away from opportunities that are not profitable or are a waste of time. This frees you to walk *toward* prospects that have full budgets and are committed to investing in your products and services.

Conviction and Confidence

Salespeople claim they bring high value to customers because of their personal expertise and commitment to service. They boast that they are working for the number one company in the industry. Testimonials from satisfied clients fill their websites and brochures. So if the salesperson believes she is the best and her company is the best, why is that same salesperson so quick to discount? Perhaps her sales and marketing rhetoric is empty and she lacks the confidence and conviction in her ability and her company's value.

Years ago, when I was a vice president of sales, I received a valuable lesson on the importance of conviction from one of my sales reps. We sold athletic wear to schools and part of the product offering was tennis shoes. It was a very competitive business.

We were not the only distributor of certain brands of tennis shoes, and often competed with small mom-and-pop stores that could undercut our prices due to low overhead. Other competitors used tennis shoes as a loss leader to gain entry into an account.

Jamie, one of my Florida reps, was outselling everyone in this product category. Even better, she was selling our highest-priced shoe at full margin. Her sales were all the more impressive because other salespeople across the country claimed they could only sell the shoes if we offered a significant discount or threw a freebie into the purchase. In many cases, we lowered our prices to win and retain the business.

After analyzing sales, I presumed that Jamie had developed a very persuasive sales presentation or value proposition. I called her, hoping to learn more about her approach in order to share it with the rest of the team. The answer was surprisingly short and easy.

"Well, I don't know exactly what I am saying or doing," she said. "I just don't give them an option on pricing since I know I will offer them the best service and so will the company. And the reason I can sell the high-priced shoes is because I don't even mention the cheaper ones. These shoes offer a better value and will last longer, wouldn't you agree?"

Jamie's simple logic is a classic demonstration of how belief in yourself, your company, and your product wins over any complicated pricing or discount strategy. It's called self-regard. Jamie was confident of her ability to deliver high value, and that confidence was better than any selling script. If you are not convinced you bring value, why should a customer pay your price? Jamie unknowingly was also applying the "walk-away" sales principle. She was willing to walk from business that wasn't open to paying full price for her product and service.

Another story about conviction comes from a colleague in the sales training business. This gentleman had only been in the business two years when we met at a conference. He was very excited, as he had just sold his first keynote presentation. He was especially excited because he asked and received $15,000 for his one-hour presentation.

My jaw dropped when I heard this, because people commanding those fees generally have a bestselling book, have been in the business for a decade or more, or are a recognized thought leader in a particular industry. He was none of the above. My colleague's conviction and confidence are what allowed him to ask and receive top speaking fees. He wasn't cocky, but he had high self-regard and was confident of his ability to deliver results. Soft skills put hard dollars in his pocket.

Action Steps for Improving Your Ability to Get Paid What You Are Worth

The checkbook stage can be a challenging one to master because it's often misdiagnosed. Salespeople naturally focus on improving hard selling skills to improve outcomes, not realizing that lack of soft skills is equally important in getting paid what you are worth. We always recommend you examine both in order to diagnose and improve your results.

Most salespeople are not aware of their money talk that follows them into adulthood. Many are not aware of negotiation tactics designed to get a salesperson emotional. Some are not convinced of the value they bring to their clients. The result is that they waste time and money with prospects who are not willing or able to invest in their services.

Here are three steps to help you conquer this selling stage and earn the revenues that you work hard for and deserve:

1. Identify your emotional triggers regarding money.

2. Educate yourself on negotiation tactics.

3. Examine your convictions about the value of your company and your own abilities.

Step #1: Identify Your Emotional Triggers Regarding Money

Think about how you handle money conversations with your prospects and customers. What statements, questions, or objections from them trigger a response that results in you discounting your fees? How do you respond when prospects say they don't have a budget or they are not willing to share it with you? Do you go into flight mode and write up yet another practice proposal? Do you revert back to the age of six and apply your childhood money scripts?

Once you identify the triggers, work on changing your response by visualizing and practicing better answers. See yourself being assertive and asking for what you need. Schedule downtime and ask yourself a few questions. What's driving your response? Is it fear of losing the business (even when it's not profitable business)? Are you worried you will offend the prospect by being assertive and asking for what you need?

Purchase a book that helps you recognize self-limiting beliefs about money. We often recommend the *Secrets of the Millionaire Mind: Mastering the Inner Game of Wealth* (HarperBusiness, 2005) by T. Harv Eker because it aligns philosophically with our beliefs as to why salespeople don't reach their earning potential. We especially like one of Eker's wealth principles: "Consciousness is observing your thoughts and actions so you can live from true choice in the present rather than being run by programming from the past."

Apply basic common sense. For example, would you like working with a real estate agent who kept showing you houses out of your price range? Or would you rather work with one who asked your budget and invested her time in showing you what you wanted, needed, and could afford?

Treat your prospects with that same respect and have conversations with them about their budgets before wasting everyone's time with recommendations they can't afford or use.

Step #2: Educate Yourself on Negotiating Tactics

Author and Poet Maya Angelou said, "When you know better, you do better." Learn about yourself and your money talk. Learn to recognize and handle negotiating tactics by enrolling in a workshop. Sophisticated buyers have been trained in negotiation skills so it's important that you show up to meetings equally prepared to engage in creating win-win outcomes for you and your company.

KARASS seminars, founded by Dr. Chester Karass, are conducted by experts in negotiation skills training. Dr. Karass says, "In business as in life, you don't get what you deserve, you get what you negotiate."

Here are a few useful negotiating tips from Dr. Karass. Note the emotional intelligence skills involved.

- ► Take the win-win approach to negotiations to find a better deal for both parties. (*Interpersonal relationships.*)
- ► Lose the need to be liked and get used to conflict. (*Emotion management.*)
- ► Practice good listening skills—always. (*Problem solving and empathy.*)
- ► Always test the resolve of the other party. (*Reality testing.*)

Remember: When you know better, you do better.

Step #3: Examine Your Convictions about the Value of Your Company and Your Own Abilities

If you forget or have doubts about your value, ask your best clients what has changed or improved for them due to working with you or your company. The conversation will remind you of the value you bring that you may be taking for granted. It helps increase your self-confidence and conviction, which makes you more comfortable discussing price and value with future prospects. Keep a "brag folder" in your office. Fill it with testimonials, case studies, and thank-you notes, reminders of the value you bring.

Raise your self-awareness of your relationship to money. Identify triggers that lower your price, value, and commissions. Get your prospects to "show you the money" before you write up a proposal or recommendation.

And always, value yourself and what you bring to your clients.

CHAPTER 9

People Over Process

The Key Traits of Emotionally Intelligent Sales Cultures

THE GOAL of sales organizations is to grow profitable, sustainable revenues. To make this happen, CEOs and sales managers watch trends in the market to learn where to invest future time and energy. They analyze existing customers to determine account penetration and up-selling opportunities. They compile prospect lists, develop pursuit strategies, study the competition to expose gaps in their offerings, and evaluate marketing and sales collateral to make sure messaging statements are on target.

These are all best practices that will increase sales. But there is also another way to increase sales that is often overlooked or undervalued. If you want to dramatically and permanently change your sales results, change your sales culture.

The relevant definition in the *Merriam-Webster Dictionary* defines culture as "the set of shared attitudes, values, goals, and practices that characterizes an institution or an organization." A culture determines how you treat your employees, serve your clients, and contribute to the community at large. A good sales culture will make you money.

Strong, emotionally intelligent sales cultures share three common traits: they promote learning, value collaboration, and encourage generosity.

To promote learning, they practice self-actualization, always encouraging members of their team to engage in personal and professional improvement. They offer employees education and training and treat this training as an investment, rather than as a line-item expense. They believe that an educated salesperson is more successful and fulfilled in his work.

GE is probably the most famous example of a learning culture. GE's John F. Welch Leadership Center, better known as Crotonville, is built on a fifty-three-acre campus. It's the leading edge of organizational development, leadership, innovation, and change. At GE, the employees know that the learning never stops. Three times a year GE's Corporate Audit Staff from sites around the globe gather to attend a two-week Leadership Training program where, for twelve hours a day for five days each week they do case study work in addition to receiving training in technical writing, branding, and communication skills. The company invests about $1 billion every year on training and education programs. Not coincidentally, GE finished with revenues of $147.3 billion in 2011.

Continued training not only leads to bigger revenues, but also to improved employee retention. Most pundits today tell business owners that long-term retention of employees is unattainable. "You can only expect a person to stay with your company two years—then they will leave," they claim. "People are just not loyal to their employers anymore." This isn't the case with our clients who have built strong sales cultures. One of the reasons they hold onto their salespeople is their investment of time and money in their staff. Educated salespeople bring in more revenue. Nice commission checks in addition to a pleasant environment make for happy salespeople and increased retention.

Collaboration is another common trait in high-performing sales cultures. Teamwork is a core value in these cultures; they work hard to make sure that each member of the sales team is helping other members. Self-centered salespeople need not apply at these organizations.

Emotionally intelligent sales cultures recognize that it takes a "sales village" to compete in today's competitive business environment. They are aware that departments such as accounting, legal, fulfillment, customer service, and marketing are just as important as the sales department in helping the company achieve its revenue goals. Everyone plays a role in acquiring and retaining clients. And that contribution is recognized and appreciated.

Generosity is the final common trait found in emotionally intelligent sales cultures. They are givers, not takers. Socially responsible, they give back to each other and their communities. These companies have discovered that giving generates goodwill that seems to add to both the top and bottom line.

Up to this point in the book we've focused on how emotional intelligence skills impact a salesperson's ability to open and close business effectively and profitably. We've discussed specific attributes that are important to use during certain selling stages.

In this chapter, we shift the focus to how these skills can help companies build winning cultures that motivate salespeople and other employees. Whether you are a salesperson or a sales leader, you can make a difference in creating and supporting an emotionally intelligent sales culture.

Skills such as self-actualization, self-awareness, social responsibility, interpersonal communication, and empathy help companies and their employees build effective teams. They promote collaboration and encourage the kind of community involvement that enhances an organization's profile and success. Let's look at how emotional intelligence helps to build a winning sales culture.

Are You Learning or Lagging?

"How's business?" Due to the recession that began in 2008, we've been asked this question more than once in the past few years. We are always happy to answer, "It's very good." The next question we're asked is, "Well, how about your clients?" And the answer is similar: "Our clients are doing pretty well."

One of the reasons we believe that our company and our clients are doing well is that all of us pursue continuous improvement. We are lifelong learners—and so are our clients.

Lifelong learning sales organizations invest in personal and professional development in good times and bad. They believe the Maya Angelou quote we mentioned in Chapter 8: "When people know better, they do better." When employees learn about exercise and nutrition, for example, they feel healthy and are more productive. When they are trained in techniques to handle adversity, they are prepared when a volatile economy hits. They are ready for battle when tough times appear.

After the 2008 financial disaster, many sales organizations that were not on the path of continuous improvement were ill prepared for battle. They found themselves staring at empty sales pipelines. Their customers had either gone out of business, were ordering fewer products, or, for the first time in years, were sending the business out to bid. Many sales teams had simply gotten out of the habit of consistent prospecting. These teams faced six to eight months of rebuilding their sales pipelines.

This new business environment also found salespeople facing heavy competition. Instead of three companies competing for a project, there were suddenly ten to twenty. Average selling skills and skills that were rusty or just plain outdated were not winning business in this competitive climate. This lack of skills enhancement and sales activity sharply affected these companies' cash flow and the reps' commissions. And in more than a few cases, businesses closed their doors.

By contrast, sales organizations that had invested in training all along were disciplined and continued to prospect, even during the prosperous times. They had full sales pipelines because they didn't fall into the bad habit of waiting for the phone to ring or email to ping. They consistently worked on honing, upgrading, and refining their selling skills so that when tough times hit, they were ready to go, not just starting to prepare for battle.

While it wasn't always easy, sales organizations that stressed ongoing learning made it through the recession in much better shape than their competitors.

Jerry Stead, CEO of IHS, a global information company based in Denver, Colorado, has experienced enormous success during his business career. We had the good fortune of hearing him speak a couple of years ago. During his presentation, he shared one of his many success philosophies. "If I had only one dollar left to spend," he told the audience, "I'd invest it in training and development for my people." This is a man who believes in lifelong learning. And that philosophy has served him well. Under his leadership, IHS has experienced 20 percent compounded growth per year for the last ten years.

Are You Getting Smarter?

In addition to navigating a challenging and volatile economy, your company has probably experienced many changes in recent years that require your employees to learn new information and/or skills. For example, your business has likely been affected by:

- ▶ Global expansion, creating a new pool of customers that often require new approaches and selling techniques.

- ▶ More companies bidding on the same work, elevating the need for your staff to know how to sell value rather than price.

- ▶ New methods for marketing services, necessitating the need to learn the ins and outs of social media.

- ▶ New technologies to communicate with prospects and clients, including such tools as desktop video conferencing and texting.

- ▶ Shorter deadlines for delivering information and products, demanding quicker response time and results.

Are you and your sales team smarter than you were two years ago? Salespeople who do not possess self-actualization skills will be very frustrated in today's rapidly changing business environment. Their lack of desire and motivation to learn and improve puts them way behind competitors who aggressively pursue self-improvement.

In his well-known book *Future Shock* (Random House, 1984), first published in 1970, futurist and bestselling author Alvin Toffler said this in regard to learning: "The illiterate of the future are not those who cannot read or write. They are those who cannot learn, unlearn and relearn."

This is a great quote to live by. Sales organizations seeking a competitive edge in a tough business environment can do so by creating learning environments. Is your culture one of learning or are you lagging behind in personal and professional development?

Case Study

Some years ago, we were hired by a company that had three divisions with three separate sales managers. Our approach to sales and sales management was embraced by the sales managers of two of the three divisions. The sales manager in the third division, however, had no interest in self-actualization. He was rigid and stuck in his way of doing things.

He politely told us that we really didn't understand his business, explaining that sales was only about relationships. Our "fancy training" that focused on setting expectations, asking questions, and analyzing the return on investment for buyers was just a little too formal for his taste.

This gentleman was in denial about the changes taking place in business and what customers want and expect from a salesperson. Yes, customers value relationships, but they also value a sales consultant who possesses business acumen and critical-thinking skills. It isn't an either/or proposition. A relationship-building dinner is wonderful. But we find that the happiest clients are those who leave a dinner meeting with their mind and stomach equally full.

This manager's lack of buy-in trickled down to the team, and they pushed back on every idea and skill we taught. We sat down with the president and shared our concern about the sales manager's unwillingness to buy into a new way of selling. The president was a long-time friend of the sales manager, so he was reluctant to give him an ultimatum. Five years later, this division lost thousands of dollars in sales to a competitor whose team had embraced a consultative sales approach. The president was finally forced to fire his long-time colleague.

We don't tell you this story to elevate ourselves and say, "We told you so," but because we see this scenario more than we'd like. We tell our clients that the only time you can afford not to change, grow, or improve is when your competitor has made the same decision.

The Mastery Gap

So why don't sales organizations and salespeople pursue personal and professional development? Besides denial and aversion to change, there is another reason. We call it the "mastery gap."

In order to understand the mastery gap, let's consider a sales-person who is trying to learn new selling skills. The salesperson's current neural pathways and habits are wired to use old sales tech-niques she has used hundreds of times. They are familiar and com-fortable. When she tries to learn and use new sales skills, however, inevitably her first attempts are uncomfortable. She knows what to do, but is not yet masterful at employing what she has learned. This gap produces an emotional response and she feels frustrated and perhaps even a little embarrassed.

Negative self-talk kicks in and the salesperson begins to rational-ize reasons for going back to her old ways. "That new sales approach doesn't work in my world," she says. "I sound canned and disingen-uous." Even though the old skills resulted in her client's price-shopping her services while she chased uninterested buyers and met with the wrong decision makers, the techniques felt comfortable. That longing for comfort draws her back into her old way of doing things. She doesn't work through the gap between knowing and mas-tering the new approach.

Her sales manager isn't helpful in pulling her through this. He teaches a new skill once and then expects the sales team to execute it flawlessly. He gets irritated when the salesperson doesn't learn new selling skills as quickly as he did. He doesn't have enough time to spend on role-playing and skill drills. He gets frustrated and rationalizes that the old approach was getting decent, if not stellar results. Soon, both the salesperson and sales manager give up and settle for the status quo, hoping that the competitor gets just as frus-trated when trying to learn new skills.

When faced with the mastery gap, you need to make a decision as to whether or not you are ready to leave your old, comfortable ways behind. This decision requires the emotional intelligence skills of self-awareness and the ability to delay gratification.

Be aware of the self-talk that persuades you to settle for being average and not achieving your full potential. Evaluate your desire for instant results. Are you giving in to the pull of instant gratifica-tion? Apply your delayed-gratification skills and put in the work necessary to achieve the reward of mastery. Close the gap between knowing and doing and continue on your journey of improvement.

There Is No "I" in Team

Sales cultures that encourage self-improvement understand that every member of the company contributes to the whole. They promote the idea that everyone works for the same team. When you study great teams, whether sales or athletic, you find that most of them enjoy success because they practice what Michael Jordan, one of the NBA's greatest players, preaches: "There is no 'I' in team, but there is in win."

Emotionally intelligent sales cultures promote teamwork and collaboration. Unfortunately, there are still many sales organizations that harbor the belief that top sales producers work outside of the team. They promote the attitude that these salespeople are difficult by their very nature and that they should be forgiven for their high-maintenance behavior. *"It just goes with the territory,"* management tells itself.

We call these high-maintenance salespeople "Lone Sales Rangers." These individuals don't worry about how their actions affect other departments; they are only concerned about getting the deal done. They often overpromise on delivery dates, putting unnecessary strain on other departments. They don't like to participate or contribute during sales meetings because they are concerned about one thing only: themselves.

Prior to the information age, sales organizations could get by hiring and keeping Lone Sales Rangers, but the Internet has changed the sales game. Today, salespeople face a more competitive environment. Company size no longer matters; small companies appear big with a great-looking website or proactive social media campaigns. Competition is no longer local. It's regional, national, and international—all accessible online. Finally, as discussed in

Chapter 1, prospects are armed with more information than ever before. They research you and your products on the Web before even having a conversation or meeting.

Sales organizations that desire to thrive in this competitive business climate know they can't afford to have Lone Sales Rangers on their team. They hire and attract team players who are willing to share best practices, mentor new sales reps, and help other members on their team close business. These organizations and their team players understand that it takes a "sales village" to compete and win in today's business environment.

Delete the "I" and Promote the "We"

There are many ways to eliminate the "I" in your sales culture and promote the team. The first is by encouraging your strongest producers to help fellow members of the sales team. This can be a challenge for some competitive salespeople who secretly don't want their team members to get better because they like being the top sales dog.

If you have that attitude, allow us to be blunt: stop being stupid! Your team member is not your competition. Your competition is the company down the street, on the Internet, or overseas. The more market share those companies take, the bigger their reputations and the more difficult your job as a salesperson becomes.

Salespeople willing to contribute to a group possess the emotional intelligence skill of social responsibility. As introduced in Chapter 1, social responsibility is the ability to be a cooperative and constructive member of your social group even if you don't benefit personally.

This type of salesperson understands that their contribution could help their peers elevate their selling skills, become more professional, and become more likeable. As a result, their organization's reputation will be enhanced. They do it because they are nice people and also because these salespeople want to surround themselves with the best. They know that the best quarterback doesn't win the Super Bowl; the best team does.

We recently worked with a sales team that was competing against each other more than against their competition. After our "stupid" speech, we helped them rethink their core values and learn the power of teamwork. To their credit, the team understood and bought into this principle. A good example of this involved one of the sales reps who was knocking her quota out of the park. She qualified early for the company incentive trip and was on her way to earning a nice bonus. She was not only a great salesperson but also a great team player and turned over a good lead to a fellow salesperson. He closed the deal, helping him qualify for the incentive trip, too.

In their book *The Orange Revolution* (Free Press, 2010), best-selling authors and leadership consultants Adrian Gostick and Chester Elton examine breakthrough teams. Their research shows that these teams are sincerely interested in helping each other achieve. They sum it up with a great word: cheer. These teams cheer for one another.

Are members of your sales team cheering for other members, or are they wasting time and energy competing with members of their own team? Are they sharing their brilliance and insights, or are they keeping all the knowledge to themselves?

As a Lone Sales Ranger, you cannot achieve your company's goal of hitting 10 to 30 percent growth for the next ten years. It takes a group. There is no "I" in team. Cheer for your team and encourage others to do the same.

Working with Your Village

To work effectively as a team, members must understand the challenges other team members face. Salespeople who aren't familiar with each department's role in delivering the end product or service are not much value to their company or customers. Companies who don't encourage this kind of awareness among employees are likely to experience destructive logjams and work blockages.

In many organizations, conflict often arises between Operations and Sales. The salesperson brings in the deal and Operations is frustrated. The deal lacks critical information, overpromises commitments, or contains inaccurate pricing. For his part, the salesperson believes these other departments—which he dubs "the sales prevention departments"—exist just to make sure his deal doesn't get done. "Those people" just don't understand the difficulty of getting a deal in the door.

If you identify with this scenario, you need to realize that relationship building starts at home. It's time to apply soft skills to your internal customers—your team members. Use your interpersonal skills to learn more about your peers in other departments. Good sales teams improve results by learning their prospect's story; many would experience the same success if they took the same amount of time to learn their fellow team members' stories.

Take "those people" out to lunch. Ask questions about their lives outside of work. Do they have kids? What do they do for fun? Where did they grow up? When you learn someone's story, you may discover the reasons behind their behavior or attitude. Maybe they are grumpy because they are caring for aging parents or a sick child. Or perhaps they're just shy—not aloof or stuck up, as you may have first thought.

Find out what their daily work life is like. Show empathy and interest. What challenges do they face in their job? Are they lacking resources to get their job done? Who else and what else demands their time and energy? What can you do to make their job easier?

When we ask salespeople these questions about their fellow team members, we often hear, "I don't know. I didn't think to ask." What the salesperson is really saying is, "I don't care." When you don't care about others, they don't go the extra mile to help you achieve your goals. Work as hard on being likeable in the office as you do with your customers.

Case Study

Kristen, a new vice president of sales, felt like she was banging her head against the wall trying to work with her company's IT department. She felt like they were not listening or responding to her requests for various sales reports needed to improve forecasting.

She listened to our advice and applied her interpersonal skills. She took the director of IT out to lunch and asked questions about his personal and professional life. She gained a new understanding of what life was like in the IT department and was surprised to learn that other departments made as many demands on IT as she did. The IT director had to balance these multiple requests along with a long list from the CEO.

As a result of getting to know her colleague's world, Kristen evaluated her requests and cut her IT wish list in half. When she did make a request, she took time to explain why it was important and the impact it would have on the entire company. Her empathy and interpersonal skills paid off. She was no longer just another person making a request. She was a trusted person that took the time to walk a mile in her co-worker's shoes. As a result, her requests were more thoughtful and IT was more responsive.

Take time to uncover your colleagues' stories. In the process, your peers will also learn your story. Members of other departments often think salespeople have it easy. They imagine days filled with lunches, dinners, and golf. Few understand the grind of travel or the pressure and risk taking required to succeed in a job in which you don't get paid unless you sell something. Many don't realize the skill it takes to influence buyers and close business.

One of our clients requires new salespeople to sit in their company's customer service department for two full days as part of their training. After witnessing nonstop calls, salespeople have a new appreciation for the skill and emotion management required to deal with often-difficult clients.

This client also requires the customer service rep to spend two days in the field with a sales rep. The customer service person quickly sees another side of the business. When he finds himself driving to an early morning appointment at 6:30 A.M. and wrapping up with a prospect dinner at 10:00 P.M., he realizes that the "glamour" of sales is not so glamorous. After these exercises, both the customer service representative and the salesperson have empathy *and* respect for one another's roles.

Don't make assumptions that people are simply out to make your life difficult: walk a few yards in your colleagues' shoes.

The Power of Gratitude

Once you've built these relationships with your co-workers, don't fall into the bad habit of taking people for granted again. This reminds us of the old joke in which the wife complains to her husband that he never says "I love you" anymore. And the husband replies, "I told you I loved you twenty years ago. Nothing has changed."

You write thank-you notes to your clients for their business, so why not write notes to members of your internal team expressing your gratitude for their contributions? Though salespeople are the most visible talent in a company and often receive more recognition, employees in other departments contribute significantly to the company as well. You sold it, but someone else is going to ship it, service it, and invoice it.

When you receive an "atta boy" from one of your customers or a thank-you note, share the recognition with other departments. Make it a priority to point out the good work of others in meetings. When a co-worker is particularly helpful to you, send an email to that person's boss. Buy a small gift of appreciation.

Here's one thing you can be certain of: no one in your organization goes home complaining about being overappreciated.

There are many people in an organization to whom you can show gratitude. Take time to write a note to your sales manager, thanking him for making you stretch your skills and achieve more than you thought possible, or for helping you set goals and holding you accountable to them. Show appreciation for the tough job a sales manager faces as he wears the multiple hats of coach, trainer, and corporate executive.

Don't forget about your CEO. It's lonely at the top and she makes decisions and takes risks every day. Send a note letting her know how much you appreciate the wisdom and hard work she puts in creating a financially stable company, one that feeds many families. Don't forget to thank her as well for the things many employees take for granted, such as benefits.

Have your sales team pen a note of thanks to the vendors at your company. Could any of you work without office supplies? How about technology assistance? Do you have someone who caters food to your company on a regular basis? Subcontractors? They are all part of your team.

When Nick, our "IT guy," shared the news of his newborn son, we shipped out a little congratulations package. Nick has helped us during the workweek, even when we didn't have a scheduled appointment. He has come in on weekends to troubleshoot issues. We appreciate his service because when he keeps our technology up and running, he is helping us be more productive.

Make gratitude a habit in your sales organization. The formula for success here is pretty simple: when people feel valued and part of the big picture, they work harder to improve that big picture.

It's Better to Give

Not only do emotionally intelligent sales cultures work well as a team, but they also see the value of generosity—of contributing on a larger scale. High-performing businesses have a strong sense of social responsibility. They believe in giving back to the communities that support them.

Are these organizations able to give back because they are doing well? Or are they doing well because they are giving back? We believe it's the latter. We've found that most successful organizations had a spirit of giving *before* they experienced their current success.

Look no further than your backyard and you will find some remarkable examples. OtterBox®, based in Fort Collins, Colorado, is one such company located near us. OtterBox makes durable covers for technology such as smart phones and tablets. They have enjoyed a 3,179 percent growth over the past three years.

CEO Curt Richardson says, "Giving back is a big part of our culture and belief system. We live by the saying, 'To whom much is given, much is expected.'" The company established the Otter-Cares^{SM} Foundation, focused on helping youth. In 2011, they awarded grants to more than 100 nonprofit organizations and events in northern Colorado. Every employee is also given twenty-four hours of paid time to volunteer and help out the charity of their choice. OtterBox has a great product. They also have a great culture.

PCL Construction Enterprises, with the U.S. headquarters based in Denver, Colorado, posts revenue of $6 billion annually. PCL focuses on relationships within the communities in which it serves and as a result, continues to do well, even when most construction firms have taken a huge economic hit. Each "PCLer" finds unique ways to be involved and support those who are less fortunate.

President and COO Peter Beaupre says, "Giving back to the community and being part of our community is rooted in our culture." The U.S. division of PCL supported charitable organizations in 2011 by donating approximately $3.5 million in total. This "giving back" mindset takes on a whole new meaning and level of impact because PCL is 100 percent employee owned. This means that donations come directly from employees' checkbooks. A portion of the dollars that could be directed to personal financial gain are instead donated to charities, with which PCL employees are often personally involved.

You don't have to be a large corporation with deep pockets to embrace the give-back philosophy. Nonprofits are always in need of volunteers who are willing to donate their time and talent. As part of your compensation plan, give employees one or two days off to devote to helping those less fortunate.

In addition to contributing to your company's public profile, the gesture will reap other benefits. For example, giving back is a very quick way to put your sales life in perspective. When you are serving dinner to people who have lost their homes, you don't feel so bad about the sale you lost that day. When you help a person without a job, it's pretty hard not to be grateful for yours. And cold calling seems like a walk in the park after you hear a child's story of overcoming abuse by a parent.

It is better to give. Research shows that people enjoy working for companies that pursue profits *and* purpose. Is your sales culture one of giving or just receiving?

Action Steps for Building Emotionally Intelligent Sales Cultures

You work eight to ten hours every day, so why not aim to create a work environment where people say, "I get to go to work," rather than, "I have to go to work"?

Cultures that energize people have a buzz and excitement to them. People like what they do, know what to do, get training on how to do it better, and work with people who have their best interests in mind. Sales teams in these types of companies foster cooperative and self-actualizing behavior in their employees. Here are four steps to help you become a valuable member of your team and enhance your organization's culture at the same time:

1. Create a learning environment.
2. Get rid of the "I's."
3. Recognize and appreciate the efforts of others.
4. Contribute to your community.

Step #1: Create a Learning Environment

Start small and create a book- or audio-of-the-month club with your team. Then choose good sales and personal development titles as the club's focus. During your weekly sales meetings, discuss key takeaways from these books and how the author's ideas can be applied to the group members' professional and personal lives. Think of training and development as an investment, not an expense. Do the math and apply the principle of compounding. Once your sales team has learned a new skill, you will enjoy the benefits of this for many years. Improved sales margins, better cash flow, and repeat business can all be connected to building a smarter sales team.

Step #2: Get Rid of the "I's"

Time is our most valued asset, which is why many of us are reluctant to share it. As salespeople, we are paid for performance, so why would we want to take the newbie out to lunch? It takes away valuable time that could be spent selling or servicing our clients.

The reasons are many. No doubt someone helped you when you were just beginning your career. Tap into your social responsibility and help others. Take the new kid on the block out to lunch. Share with him some tips that will decrease his ramp-up time. If you have a colleague that has hit a slump, offer to go on a sales call just to observe and/or assist. We've all experienced slumps and a "little help from friends" is appreciated.

A sales organization is only as good as its weakest link. Everyone needs to hit their sales goals in order for the company to consistently achieve its larger revenue goals.

Step #3: Recognize and Appreciate the Efforts of Others

Sam Walton, founder of Walmart, says: "Appreciate everything your associates do for the business. Nothing else can quite substitute for a few well-chosen, well-timed, sincere words of praise. They're absolutely free and worth a fortune."

We'll say it again: it takes a sales village. Even in very small businesses, non-salespeople contribute greatly to the company's success and reputation. Consider the person answering the phone, for example. This is the first point of contact for your prospects and clients. Thank this person for making a good first impression. Let her know how much you appreciate her warmth in engaging customers and making them feel important and welcome.

Organized and effective salespeople make to-do lists and goals for the week. Put one more item on your to-do list: recognizing and thanking someone every day. Salespeople with good interpersonal skills make it a goal to be the "Kudos King or Queen" in their organization. They know that appreciation never goes out of style.

Step #4: Contribute to Your Community

You might be reading this thinking, "Well, my company isn't that philanthropic; no one wants to hear my ideas about how to help the community." This may be so, but it doesn't matter. Quit waiting for someone else to be the change agent. Make it your cause to get your sales organization or company to be generous and get involved in charitable and community work.

Emotionally intelligent sales organizations pursue both purpose and profits. As Gandhi so eloquently said, "Be the change you want to see in the world." Start making changes to build a strong sales culture now. Promote learning, teamwork, and giving back to others. When you have an organization that embraces these behaviors, you have people who enjoy each day of selling—and succeed as a result.

CHAPTER 10

Take the Lead

Sales Leadership and Emotional Intelligence

YOU'VE LIKELY HEARD this story before: Tom is a hard-working salesperson who is a student of his profession. He becomes the top producer at the company and, because of his outstanding sales results, is promoted into management.

But in his new position as a sales leader, Tom quickly becomes puzzled and frustrated because his team isn't hitting its revenue goals. In order to make sure the company goals are met, he is forced to put his salesperson hat back on. Due to this dual role, he is now working seven days a week and is beginning to question his decision to move into management. Self-doubt sets in. How could he be so successful as a salesperson, only to fail miserably as a sales leader?

The answer is simple. The tasks Tom excelled at as a top sales producer are very different from the tasks needed to lead a high-performance sales team. A salesperson is responsible for developing sales opportunities, whereas a sales manager is responsible for developing people. A top salesperson succeeds with good selling skills, while an effective sales manager must also excel at *teaching* the selling skills and knowledge that made him successful.

Is it any wonder that salespeople often have trouble transitioning into the role of sales manager?

When we conduct sales management training workshops, we ask participants to think about effective leaders, coaches, or mentors they've had in their lives. Then, we ask them to write down specific attributes that made these people effective in their roles.

The answers often include: "He cared about me." "She really made me stretch." "He was a great teacher." "She was disciplined and focused." "He didn't accept excuses." While varied, the answers are similar in one important way: None of them focus on hard skills. No one says: "He was good at accounting." "She was a manufacturing genius." "He was brilliant at technology." It's soft skills that make up the most critical part of the success equation.

No doubt many of you reading this book are sales producers who aspire to be in management or have already attained that level. If so, you need soft skills such as impulse control, empathy, self-awareness, delayed gratification, and interpersonal skills to improve your ability to lead and develop others.

Let's take a look at the roles and responsibilities of a sales manager and the associated emotional intelligence skills that can enhance your success as a sales leader. We will examine your need to act consistently, offer inspiration and guidance, set high expectations, and recognize the efforts of those on your team.

How Do You Show Up?

Most everyone would agree that consistency is an important trait for a leader. At a basic level, consistency is connected to self-awareness and impulse control. Effective leaders must be aware of their emotions in order to manage them. Without such awareness, a leader can react to events that occur during the course of a day and behave in a manner that is not congruent with stated values, words, or actions. Such behavior rapidly erodes trust and credibility.

Inconsistent behavior is often due to poor impulse control. The manager says or does things without fully thinking through the impact of her words or actions, allowing events of the day to affect her emotions.

During the Monday morning sales meeting, for example, the sales manager is in a good mood and praises the team for their efforts and results. She gives a small pep talk on the topics of respect and personal accountability, emphasizing the importance of these traits in achieving personal and professional success.

The next day, after a tough meeting with the CEO, she turns irate, pressuring the team to sell more—or else. This behavior is the exact opposite of her pep talk from the day before. The team doesn't know if they can believe or trust her because the message is always changing.

We call this kind of leader a "fair weather" sales manager. She's nice as long as everything is going well. But when a business storm is brewing, this manager is the first to lose her cool. She becomes part of the problem, not the solution. Her temper flares, she points fingers, and she lets accusations fly—all due to her inability to manage her emotions.

Every day, the team asks the same question: "What kind of mood is Sarah in today?" As a result of her volatility, no one brings up current or potential problems. Salespeople don't ask for advice because they can't predict the mood of the day. Difficulties don't get resolved and skills don't improve, which affects client satisfaction, team morale, and sales revenues.

Great sales leaders excel at managing their emotions and don't allow daily events to affect what they do or how they do it. They choose how they want to show up. We call these sales managers "all weather" leaders. They are capable of handling any kind of business storm without losing control.

If a major competitor moves into town, the manager doesn't hit the panic button. She reminds the team that competition is good because it prevents complacency. If internal operations issues are impacting sales results, she doesn't yell at other department heads. She works on getting the issues fixed, even when it's not her department's responsibility.

As the sales team observes her calm demeanor, they learn they can trust their manager to react in predictable ways that reflect self-control, respect for others, and proactive thinking.

How do you show up every day? Are you an "all weather" or a "fair weather" leader?

Do Your Words and Actions Align?

In addition to inconsistent behavior, one of the quickest ways to destroy credibility and integrity as a sales leader is to say one thing and do another. The words and actions don't align. Remember, your team watches what you do more than they listen to what you say.

Consider a sales manager who preaches the importance of being on time to meetings with clients and prospects. He emphasizes the need for having a defined objective for each meeting and stresses the importance of preparation. Yet when he holds the weekly sales meeting, he models neither of the above. He arrives late and allows reps to straggle in throughout the meeting, disrupting the flow of conversation. He doesn't distribute a written agenda of the meeting, so his sales team is not prepared to contribute and engage. The meeting quickly turns into a rote review of sales activity and pipeline. Little or no time is invested in attitude or skills training. The sales leader models the following concepts, based on his actions:

- ▶ It's acceptable to be late to a meeting.
- ▶ Agendas are not important. Go ahead and wing it.
- ▶ Preparation sounds good but probably isn't doable because of everyone's busy schedules.

Obviously, these aren't the messages most sales managers want their team members to take to heart. This manager's actions have destroyed any impact his words might have had.

A similar scenario can arise during one-on-one interactions with team members. While sales managers all agree that building relationships is important, they often demonstrate the opposite behavior.

Consider this situation: Jen meets her boss for a coaching session. She's excited to share details of a recent sales success and eager to get advice on a new opportunity she is working on. But when she begins to recount her experiences, her sales manager appears preoccupied. He takes phone calls and checks emails as he fidgets and repeatedly looks at his watch. Jen's excitement quickly fades. She doesn't feel recognized or appreciated, and the meeting ends early.

As she leaves, the sales manager says, "Thanks, Jen. I appreciate all your hard work." Jen hears the words, but remembers the manager's actions, which shouted, "Other priorities are more important than you."

Emotionally intelligent sales managers possess interpersonal skills. They value their people, and their actions support that value. Instead of preaching the importance of relationships, they *demonstrate* their importance by turning off the technology and giving you their full attention. Their words and actions align, telling you, "You're the most important priority on my agenda right now." Jen sure could have used a manager like that.

Teaching Rather Than Closing

Good sales managers do more than simply model the kind of behavior they expect from their sales team; they take an active role in helping them improve their skills. Jack Welch, former chairman of General Electric, said it best: "Before you are a leader, success is all about growing yourself. When you become a leader, success is all about growing others."

Good sales managers recognize that they are only as effective as the members on their team. Their job is no longer about opening and closing business; it's about teaching others to do so.

Sales managers who lack this awareness don't take the time to develop others. They are stuck being the company "doer," the person who closes business. The problem is that when the company reaches a certain size, there isn't enough of the sales manager to go around. She can't be at every deal. Sales stagnate or decrease because she neglected the important role of teaching others how to win business.

Teaching requires delayed-gratification skills. You must put in the time to teach and coach in order to get the reward of a self-sufficient team. This requires paying attention to what your sales staff is communicating and requesting, and then giving guidance.

To this end, the emotionally intelligent sales manager makes a decision to be fully present during meetings. He displays interest and empathy by listening and asking questions. In the previous scenario regarding Jen, a self-aware sales manager would know that his primary responsibility is to transfer his knowledge and skills to his salesperson in order to help her become a better sales professional. So instead of checking emails and taking phone calls during their meeting, he would inquire about her new opportunity, teaching her new and better ways to achieve that goal. When he offered congratulations on her recent success, the words would be specific: *"Jen, the research you did on their financials is really what made you win this project. That research shows me you took time to plan, even when it would have been easier to just 'wing' it."* As a result, Jen would feel appreciated and leave the meeting aware of what she had done right in her recent sale.

Teaching involves accompanying reps on their appointments or conducting one-on-one coaching sessions. Both can be tedious and even frustrating. ("Do I really have to show you how to do this again?") But patience pays off. In his book *What It Takes to Be #1* (McGraw-Hill, 2000), Vince Lombardi's son recounts a quote from his famous father, one of the greatest football coaches of all time, that reflects Lombardi's dedication to the role of teacher:

> They call it coaching but it is teaching. You do not just tell them it is
> so, but you show them the reason why it is so and you repeat and
> repeat until they are convinced, until they know. It was the way, back
> in Brooklyn, the good teacher I had and admired did it.

Lombardi was ahead of his time. He knew something about how the brain works and the power of repetition in mastering new skills. The "repeat and repeat" philosophy is an important one for sales managers to embrace as they teach new attitudes and skills to their teams.

Sales managers tend to fall short on this philosophy. One of the reasons for their past sales successes is that they learn new skills and acquire knowledge quickly. They count on the same from their sales teams. They teach a concept once and expect their teams to apply it flawlessly in future sales calls. In essence, what they are doing is forcing their salespeople to practice in the worst place—in front of the prospect or customer.

As we discussed in Chapter 2, new skills are learned because of the brain's ability to develop new neural pathways. But without repetition, these neural pathways atrophy and new skills are lost.

Effective sales managers control their desire for instant results. They have the patience and discipline to listen to the problems their team members are having and offer guidance. Poor sales results are often not about hard skills. The salesperson simply isn't good at handling stress, for example, or she gets anxious or critical when a sales meeting doesn't go the right way, inhibiting her ability to move forward on the next opportunity.

This is where sales managers can add valuable coaching and insights by asking a few questions:

- ➤ What's good about tough selling situations?
- ➤ What can we control or change?
- ➤ What are the lessons learned from this scenario?
- ➤ How will these lessons make you better on the next sales call?

> ▶ What's making you take the prospect's responses so personally?

These questions help the salesperson recognize that one bad sales meeting is just that.

One of the biggest differences we see between sales teams that achieve their goals and those that don't is the sales manager's involvement as teacher and coach. It's no longer about how good you are but about how good you can make others.

Tough Love, Sales Leadership Style

Leadership in sales includes letting team members know what you expect from them. This role is similar to that of a parent. Good parents set expectations of behavior and character for their children, such as: you must complete your homework before you play; you aren't allowed to text during mealtime; you are responsible for doing chores around the house. The best parents recognize that parenting is not a popularity contest, and they don't give in to comments such as *"None of the other kids' moms expect them to . . ."*

These parents are willing to hold their children to high expectations because they love them and are concerned about their welfare. They are willing to put off the instant gratification that comes from letting their kids do whatever they want because their ultimate goal is to raise successful, self-sufficient adults. And this means that when necessary, they are willing to use tough love. They make their kids abide by "the rules" even when they don't like them.

A good sales manager shows the same emotional intelligence. She cares about those on her team, and because she cares, she sets clear expectations for success. She establishes and measures key performance metrics for sales activities. Team members role-play, even when they don't like it, so they can master selling techniques. Excuses for late reports on forecasting or sales activity are not accepted.

When the sales team accuses this manager of micromanaging or having too high of expectations, she doesn't give in and lower her standards. She puts aside her need to be liked and focuses on being respected, more concerned with developing these individuals into a high-performing sales team than with being their best friend.

To do this, sales managers must possess a healthy dose of independent thinking and self-confidence. Independent thinkers are self-directed and free of emotional dependency. They know that raising the bar on performance and holding staff members accountable for results inspired the phrase, "It's lonely at the top." And because they are confident as well as independent, they don't accept excuses or mediocrity from their teams. Tough sales love creates high-performance sales cultures.

Holding Up the Mirror of Truth

Part of tough love means helping others see their own blind spots. Effective managers hold up a mirror to members of their team to show them the blemishes in their attitudes or actions.

Case Study

Karen worked for a tough-love boss who cared about her success. During an annual performance review, her boss first thanked her for her hard work and shared how proud he was that her regional team exceeded its revenue goals. Then he held up the mirror. He pointed out a flaw in her management style that disappointed him, noting that she was neglectful at building relationships in the office. Her intense focus on getting the job done often made her insensitive and rude to others. Although this feedback hit her hard, Karen is a self-aware person and a lifelong learner, so instead of ignoring the feedback she took it to heart.

The next morning she made a decision about how she wanted to show up. She realized that while she wanted to be seen as the caring person she was, she was obviously not displaying this through her actions. She began making rounds in the office, visiting other departments and thanking team members for their efforts in helping her region become number one. Karen continued this "walk-around" strategy in the ensuing months and was pleasantly surprised by how much she enjoyed these interactions. She started building her sales village.

Karen was eventually promoted to vice president of sales and led her company through amazing growth. She attributes her success to this frank conversation with her tough-love boss.

Holding the mirror up means you must be comfortable being a truth teller. And some days as a leader, that means telling a salesperson that he has a bad attitude, lacks organization, or might not be as committed to success as he claims he is. You might be the first person who has ever held up the mirror to this person. And you might be the first person who has cared enough to ask him to change and stretch in order to reach his full potential.

In the words of Tom Landry, former coach of the Dallas Cowboys, "Leadership is getting someone to do what they don't want to do, to achieve what they want to achieve."

Offering Inspiration and Recognition

Tough love doesn't mean being cruel or never showing a soft side; in fact, inspiring team members and recognizing excellence is a big part of tough love—and this is something hard-driving salespeople tend to misunderstand. Often, they land in the position of sales management because of their ability to achieve goals. They are results-oriented, which is a goal. But in keeping their eye on the goal, they can forget that managing is as much about inspiration as it is giving direction. The best sales managers recognize the accomplishments of the team and inspire members to continue to do better.

Most managers excel at problem solving. The downside is that some sales managers don't balance problem solving with praise and celebration. They only focus on pointing out what the company or sales team is doing wrong. *"Lost another one to EFG Company on price,"* a manager might say. *"We missed our delivery date to ABC Company." "MNO Company is coming out with their new product before us."* Quickly, the sales team becomes stressed and unmotivated just thinking about all the problems and challenges.

Ed Oakley and Doug Krug, co-authors of *Leadership Made Simple* (Enlightened Leadership Publications, 2006), teach a basic principle in their leadership workshops. They train leaders to open their meetings with the question, "What are we doing right?" This simple query produces powerful results. Members of the sales team begin recognizing all the good the company is doing rather than focusing on shortcomings. They begin acknowledging their own contributions and achievements, as well as those of their peers. Optimism is contagious. When each salesperson is charged with saying something positive, the sales culture moves from finding fault to finding success. The team is inspired because they begin looking for the good instead of always dwelling on what's not going right. An inspired team is a successful team.

Effective sales managers give compliments, create recognition programs, and set up events that inspire camaraderie and teamwork. Often, they reward top salespeople with material items such as rings, plaques, and incentive trips. These ideas work well as motivators, but we also recommend an often-overlooked way to recognize salespeople that is far less expensive: make them heroes.

Making someone a hero means that you pay attention and identify one thing each salesperson on your team does well. Once you have identified that "one thing," make the person a hero by pointing it out during sales meetings. If applicable, have him teach the "one thing" to his peers. This recognition establishes the salesperson as the expert and go-to person on a particular topic. It builds confidence and is an effective way to make a person feel unique and important because of his contribution.

I implemented this recognition strategy when I was vice president of sales with seven direct reports. Each person had a specific talent, the "one thing," that I recognized and developed. One manager, for instance, was especially good at selling fundraising programs. I made Lynette the "fundraising expert" at the company. Another manager was very good at selling to the youth market. Nancy became the "youth expert."

Because they were known as the experts, Lynette and Nancy invested extra time in creating programs and go-to market strategies in addition to their daily duties as sales managers. They enjoyed the stature that came with being the expert and the company reaped the rewards of these managers sharing their brilliance and creating faster growth in those product areas.

Here are a few areas of expertise that might constitute the "one thing" that a salesperson does well and can teach others:

> Creativity in business development—good at thinking outside of the box.

> Success in client retention—never loses a client.

> Ability to grow existing accounts—good at up-selling and cross-selling.

> Finesse with customer service—excellent at making lemonade out of lemons.

> Skilled in taking business away from competitors—good at finding the gap in the competitors' offering.

Make your salespeople heroes. It's a powerful form of recognition that keeps them motivated and on a journey of self-improvement.

The Most Overlooked Motivator of Them All

Finally, don't forget the most overlooked motivator of all: the fun quota. It's easy for sales managers to get caught up in the pressure of hitting monthly, quarterly, and year-end revenue goals, but everyone needs a release valve. On the surface, fun may not appear to have a direct link to hitting goals; however, if you need evidence of the correlation between fun and revenues, just study one of the most successful airlines in the business, Southwest Airlines. Fun is a core value of this organization. They hire people who have a sense of humor and use it with customers.

I was on a flight with Southwest and the flight attendant had everyone in stitches as she reviewed what is usually considered the dry rules and policies for flying. The best comment made was, "And if you are sitting by an adult that is acting like a small child, please help him administer the drop-down oxygen mask before helping yourself. It will save us all in case of an emergency landing." Southwest continues to post profits when most airlines are going out of business or into the red.

Work as hard at hitting your fun quota as you do making your sales quota. During sales meetings, show funny sales videos from YouTube. Plan a happy hour where your team can play together. Send each salesperson a humorous card once a quarter. As part of your next sales meeting, have people share tales of their worst sales calls. These stories are often hysterical and show other team members that there is life after failure.

When I was vice president of sales, we incorporated fun into the introduction of a new line of products. We rented a studio and created an audio recording to teach the reps about the new offerings in a rather unusual way: we recorded songs, poems, and skits. One skit was a serious news broadcast about the "Fleecing of America." We used the concept to introduce a new line of polar fleece jackets, discussing the potential repercussions to Americans if they didn't purchase these jackets. There could be frostbite issues due to poor coverage. Or, because they were not wearing the latest fashion, the person could possibly get arrested by the fashion police and end up in jail. And who wants to plead guilty to bad taste? All of the scenarios were ridiculous and fun.

This crazy approach worked. Reps called the corporate office, telling us they had pulled over on the side of the road because they were laughing so hard. They reported that they kept playing the audio over and over due to the humor. It was the best product launch we ever had. Having fun can make you money.

Best Practices for Sales Leadership

In reviewing the skills that make a successful sales manager, it's instructive to consider the thoughts of John Kelley, former CEO of McData Corporation and now president of CereScan. Kelley grew McData Corporation from $200 to $630 million in revenues from 2001 to 2007.

Kelley exudes emotional intelligence. After hearing him speak at an association lunch, I set up an interview specifically for this chapter of the book. I wanted to learn his secrets to leading effective sales teams and organizations. His answers support much of what has been discussed in this chapter and others. What follows is what he shared about some of his best practices.

Emotion Management

"One of the things I subscribe to and taught members of my team was [that there would be] no yelling," says Kelley. "There's no need to raise your voice. Part of the way I accomplished this was my philosophy of giving feedback fast. Deal with a problem quickly without denigrating other departments or people. When you start dwelling on something, that's when tempers can flair."

Consistency

"Good leaders come in all flavors and varieties," he notes. "However, they have a few things in common. One is that they are consistent. My best sales manager always held a Monday morning meeting that was prepared and predictable. He also planned three days in the field with his sales team. The team knew the sales manager would be looking over their account plans and calendars. That consistency and accountability produced sustainable sales results."

Self-Awareness

"It's important for people to discover for themselves that they aren't hitting the objectives or behaving in a way that is going to get them promoted," Kelley explains. He goes on to say:

> I ask five questions to help a person discover for himself that he is not on the right path.
>
>> Do you like the industry?
>>
>> Do you like your job?
>>
>> Tell me about your career path.
>>
>> Tell me the characteristics you feel are important for that career path.
>>
>> Tell me why you think you're going to get promoted based on how you're acting, as it relates to those characteristics.
>
> Usually after asking these questions, the person realized that his actions and words weren't aligning. If he wanted to go in a certain direction within the company, it was up to him or her to change.

Recognition and Appreciation

"I'm a big believer in thank-you notes," Kelley says. "When I was president of McData, I wrote five thank-you notes a day, recognizing very tangible things in the note. The notes were often a page or two because I wanted to get into the specifics of why I wanted to write the note in the first place. My desire was for the person reading the note to have an emotional connection when he read it."

In addition to tremendous growth at McData, it's worth noting that eight former members of John's team went on to become CEOs.

Action Steps for Improving Your Emotional Intelligence in Sales Leadership

We love this quote from John Maxwell, author of several bestselling leadership books (*The 21 Irrefutable Laws of Leadership, Developing the Leader Within You,* and *The 21 Indispensable Qualities of a Leader,* to mention three that have sold over a million copies each): "If you are leading, and no one is following, you are not leading. You are out for a walk."

Are you leading a highly motivated team or are you just out for a walk? As you have learned in this chapter, there is a big difference between selling and leading. Selling is more self-focused; leading is other-focused. There are five steps that will get you on the right path for leading and developing others:

1. Be consistent.
2. Give up your need to be liked.
3. Show empathy and courtesy.
4. Become a teacher.
5. Put fun on the weekly to-do list.

Step #1: Be Consistent

You give up the privilege of mood swings when you take on a leadership role. Each morning, get some downtime and think about the possible areas where you will be challenged to handle your emotions. Anticipate and visualize your calm response to those situations. Write down and repeat affirmations and questions that will help you show up the way you want. Here are a few that we suggest:

- ► *"Test your assumptions and assume your assumptions are wrong."* This phrase helps you stop jumping to conclusions and delays the impulse to say or do something incongruent with your values.
- ► *"I am calm and in control."* It's important to use the word "am" because you must act as if you have already achieved the desired behavior. The subconscious mind believes what is repeatedly affirmed, so state your desired behavior, not your current reality.
- ► *"What's funny about this?"* Sometimes it's important to lighten up and stop taking yourself and life so serious.

The pace of the leader is the pace of the group, and your ability to handle the day-to-day challenges that occur in business is key as to how your team, in turn, handles challenges.

Step #2: Give Up Your Need to Be Liked

There's a difference between liking someone and respecting them. Your sales team may like you as a person; however, they only value and apply input and feedback from people they respect.

Set high expectations for how you want your sales team to operate. Raise the bar instead of lowering it when you receive push-back on accountability. If a salesperson gives you an excuse for not executing a specific skill or activity, ask them some truth-telling questions:

- ► What did you choose to do that was more important?
- ► What's the real reason you are not calendar-blocking in order to achieve daily and weekly goals?

> ► How committed are you to your success and what proof
> are you showing me of that commitment?"

Sales managers who have a high need to be liked have a lot of friends. They also have fewer sales.

Step #3: Show Empathy and Courtesy

When you meet with a member of your sales team, pretend he is your most important customer. Would you be taking phone calls or checking email if you were meeting with a client? Show your sales team the same courtesy. Focus is a required leadership skill, and it starts with the type of interactions you have on a daily basis with your sales team. Be present, interested, and genuine. Your nonverbal expression will tell the salesperson whether or not you are present physically *and* mentally. If your answers are short and generic, he will know that you are simply checking the "meeting" box off your list. You've invested time with the person, but you have nothing to show for the investment.

Step #4: Become a Teacher

Teaching is a privilege and should not be taken lightly. You have an opportunity to make a permanent difference in a salesperson's confidence, attitude, skills, and lifestyle. Apply your delayed-gratification skills and put in the necessary time with each person on your team.

When you create your calendar for the week, write down the specific number of hours you will devote to teaching and coaching. Write down a second goal on the one thing you want your sales team to learn and focus on that week. Repeat, repeat, repeat, and you will win and win and win.

Step #5: Put Fun on the Weekly To-Do List

Take business seriously, but not yourself. Be on the lookout for small and big ways that you can add a smile, a laugh, or fun to your sales team's day. Appoint someone on your team to be the fun police. Make it their job to come up with something fun or funny that week. Sales can be stressful, so if you can provide a daily dose of stress relief, it will go a long way to making the job more enjoyable for your team.

When you are a sales leader, your team looks to you for advice, encouragement, and congruency in your words and actions. Team members rely on you to teach and guide them to become the best that they can be. Remember that salespeople work for people, not companies. Be the leader that every salesperson wants to follow.

Index

ABC (Always Be Closing), 30
Abdoo, Richard, 15–16
accountability, 114
accountability partners, 65
adversity, 57
alignment, 116–118, 182–183
Allosso, Michael, on authenticity, 71
all weather sales managers, 181, 182
Always Be Closing (ABC), 30
American Express, 10
American Society of Training and
    Development, *xvii*
amygdala, 22–24, 30
analysis, 45
analytical buyers, 131
Angelou, Maya, 158
Arden, John, on changing your brain, 22
assertiveness, 28, 101–103, 123, 138, 140
athletics, 33–34
authenticity, 70–71, 83
awareness, 37, *see also* self-awareness

Beaupre, Peter, on giving back, 175
behavior, 22
best practices, 4, 192–194
Book, Howard, 11
brain, *see* neuroscience
The Bucket List (film), 82–83
business development plans, 63–64
busy people, 45–46
buyers, 123, *see also* decision makers

Capital Value Advisors, 49
Carnegie, Dale, on making friends, 19
Cautious Thinkers, 131–133, 139
Center for Creative Leadership, 5

CEOs, 123, 174
CFOs, 123
change, 36–37, 114–116, 120–121, 178
checkbook stage, 142–159
    action steps for, 156–159
    challenges in, 143–145
    conviction and confidence for,
        154–156, 159
    dealing with strong negotiators in,
        148–149
    definition of, 142
    "money talk" in, 145–148, 157–158
    and sales pipeline, 154
    walking away during, 151–153, 156
Cialdini, Robert B., 52
closing, premature, *xi*
coaches, 65
collaboration, 162
communication, 162
communication styles, 78–80
community contributions, 178
Conceptual Age, 10
confidence, 70–71, 134–136, 154–156, 187
conflict, 158
consciousness, 157–158
consistency, 180–183, 193–195
Consortium for Research on Emotional
    Intelligence in Organizations, 10
conviction, 154–156, 159
Coolidge, Calvin, on listening, 121
cortisol, 56
courtesy, 196
Covey, Stephen, 73
Coy, Ryan, 53–54
Creedon, John, 13
culture, 160–161, *see also* sales cultures

decision makers, 122–141
  asking the right questions of, 136–138
  Cautious Thinker types of, 131–133
  committed to change, 90
  and decision making process, 124–125
  Driver types of, 125–127
  Influencer types of, 127–129
  making assumptions about, 123
  and non-decision makers, 134–136
  Steady Relator types of, 129–131
decision making, 36–37, 61, 122–123,
  140
decision making process, 124–125
delayed gratification, *xi, xii*
  with business development plans, 63
  and Cautious Thinkers, 133
  for mastery, 167–168
  in prospecting, 44–46, 48, 50
  in sales leadership, 184, 196
  as skill, *xiv*
demographics, 48
DISC communication model, 124–125,
  see also specific model types, e.g.:
  Influencers
Discover Your Sales Strengths (Benson
  Smith & Tony Rutigliano), 10
downtime, *xix,* 15–17
Drivers (personality type), 125–127, 139

EI, *see* emotional intelligence
Eker, T. Harv, on consciousness,
  157–158
Elton, Chester, 170
e-mail, 38
emotional contagion, 57
Emotional Intelligence (Daniel
  Goleman), 15–16
emotional intelligence (EI), *xi,* 3–20
  action steps for improving, 14–20
  definition of, 4–7
  and sales results, 7–14
  see also specific headings
emotional intelligence skills training,
  xiv, xv
emotionally intelligent sales cultures,
  see sales cultures

Emotional Quotient Inventory 2.0
  (EQ-i 2.0®), *xvii*
emotional triggers, 157–158
emotion management, 64–65
  and lack of buy-in, 151
  for negotiating, 158
  for sales leadership, 180–181, 192–193
emotions
  naming, 18–20
  return on, 10–12
Emotions of Normal People (William
  Moulton Marston), 125
empathy, *xiv*
  for agreeing and aligning, 117
  during checkbook stage, 153
  definition of, 19, 72–73
  for first sales meetings, 101–102
  and likeability, 72–77, 83
  in sales cultures, 162
  in sales leadership, 196
Ensign Drilling, 76–77
enthusiasm, 77–80
The EQ Edge (Steven Stein & Howard
  Book), 11
EQ-i (Reuven Bar-On Emotional Quotient Inventory), 5
EQ-i 2.0® (Emotional Quotient Inventory 2.0), *xvii*
executives, 135
expectations, 87–104
  action steps for handling, 100–104
  and chasing prospects, 87
  management of, 88, 98–100
  for partnering with clients, 88–90, 93
  in sales leadership, 186, 195
  and second meetings, 95–97
  and your mindset, 90–94
expertise, 190

fair weather sales managers, 181, 182
fans, 98–100
fear, *xi–xii*
fight-or-flight responses
  managing your, 120
  neuroscience of, 23–26, 30–31, 35
  and questioning skills, 116–118

and walking away during negotiation, 152
financial disaster of 2008, 163
flight responses, *see* fight-or-flight responses
focus, 32, 196
Ford, Henry, on thinking, 50
Franklin, Benjamin, 57
Friedman, Thomas, on agreeing with others, 117
friendliness, 83
friends, 57
fun, 191–192, 196–197
Future Shock (Alvin Toffler), 165

Gandhi, Mahatma, on change, 178
General Electric, 161
generosity, 52, 162, 174–176
"give goal," 52
Gladwell, Malcolm, 36
goals, 188–189
Goleman, Daniel, 15–16
Gostick, Adrian, 170
gratification, *see* delayed gratification; instant gratification
gratitude, 173–174, 193–194
"grunt" sales meetings, 25

Halford, Scott, *xiv,* 74
happiness, *xvi*
hard skills, 12
heroes, 189–190
high-concept skills, 10–11
high-touch skills, 12
humor, 58, 191

Imaginibbles, 94–95
impulse control, 107–108
influence, 52–53
Influence: The Psychology of Persuasion (Robert B. Cialdini), 52
Influencers, 127–129, 139
innovation, 4
insanity, 31–32
inspiration, 188–190
instant gratification, 45, 47, 132–133

interpersonal communication, 162
interpersonal skills, 124, 158
intimidation, 19
IQ, 6–7

Jazzercise, *xv–xvi*
Jerry McGuire (film), 142
Jobs, Steve, 85
Jordan, Michael, on teamwork, 168
joy, 82–84

Karass, Chester, 158
KARASS seminars, 158
Kelley, John, on leadership, 192–194
"knowing-and-doing gap," 3, 7, 26–27
Konrath, Jill, on executives, 135
KPA, 47
Krug, Doug, 189

Landry, Tom, 188
laptops, 32
Lassen, Marty, *xiv,* 74
leadership, *see* sales leadership
Leadership Made Simple (Ed Oakley & Doug Krug), 189
leading questions, 30
Learned Optimism (Martin Seligman), 13
learning
    and neuroscience, 22, 32–33, 185
    in sales cultures, 161–168, 177
likeability, 67–86
    action steps for improving, 84–86
    and enthusiasm, 77–80
    and joy giving, 82–84
    and liking yourself, 69–71
    and liking your work, 80–81
    research on, 68
    role of empathy in, 72–77, 83
    and sales leadership, 195–196
    and trust, 67
The Likeability Factor (Tim Sanders), 83
limbic system, 22–23
listening, 107–108, 121, 158
Lombardi, Vince, on teaching, 184–185
Lone Sales Rangers, 168–169

long-term memory, 26
L'Oreal, 10

Mackay, Harvey, 77
Mackay 66 (questionnaire), 77, 85
Marston, William Moulton, 125
mastery, 31, 37, 39
mastery gap, 166–168
Maxwell, John, 194
McGraw, Phil, on how people treat you, 104
memory, 26
Met Life, 13
metrics, 186
Mischel, Walter, 44–45
"money talk," 145–148, 157–158, *see also* checkbook stage
Multi-Health Systems, *xvii*
multitasking, 17

National Sales Executive Association, 45
negotiation, 144, 148–152, 158, *see also* checkbook stage
nervousness, 18–19
Nesbeth, James, 39–40
neurons, 32
neuroplasticity, 33
neuroscience, 5, 21–40
    and athletics, 33–34
    definition of, 22
    emotionally intelligent response, 27–29
    fight-or-flight response in, 23–26, 30–31, 35
    and improving your ability to influence, 35–40
    and insanity, 31–32
    and knowing-and-doing gap, 26–27
    and learning new things, 22, 32–33, 185
    of prospecting, 58–60
    role of amygdala in, 22–24, 30
No Jerk Rule, 49
non-decision makers, 134–136
Nyden, Jeanette, on negotiating, 148–149

Oakley, Ed, 189
objections, 92–94
Operations, 171
optimism, 13, 57, 189
The Orange Revolution (Adrian Gostick & Chester Elton), 170
OtterBox®, 175
Outliers (Malcolm Gladwell), 36

partnerships, client, 88–90, 93
"pattern interrupt," 117
PCL Construction Enterprises, 175–176
performance metrics, 186
personality types, 125, 139–140
Phelps, Michael, 6
Pink, Daniel, 10
planning
    with business development plans, 63–64
    pre-call, 123–124, 141
    and prospecting, 45, 49–51
practice, *xix*, 34, 39–40
pre-call planning, 123–124, 141
prefrontal cortex, 23
premature closing, *xi*
Prentice, Steve, *xix*
preparation, 71
price, 38, 142–143, *see also* checkbook stage
problem solving, 113–114, 137–138, 158, 189
productivity, 45–46
product knowledge, 3, 71
profit, *xvi*
prospecting, 43–65
    and being busy, 46
    challenges with, 43
    delayed gratification in, 44–46, 48, 50, 63
    neuroscience of, 58–60
    and planning, 45, 49–51
    with promising prospects, 47–49
    reality testing in, 54–56, 62–63
    relationship-building in, 51–53
    steps for improving, 60–65
    and stress, 56–58

prospects
 brain-hurting conversations with,
  111–112
 brain structure of, 30
 chasing, 87
 learning stories of, 121
 and likeability, 72–75
 preventing fight-or-flight responses
  from, 30–31
 see also prospecting
psychology, 5, 112–115, *see also* neuroscience
purpose, 85–86

questioning skills, 105–121
 action steps for improving, 119–121
 and commitment to change, 114–116
 and fight-or-flight responses, 116–118
 and listening, 107–108
 to make prospect's brain hurt,
  111–112
 for meetings with decision makers,
  136–138
 psychology behind, 112–115
 and verbal assault, 106
 "3Ws" approach to, 108–111, 120
questions
 asking yourself tough, 61–63
 bringing up objections with, 92–93
 leading, 30
 truth-seeking, 96, 195–196

Rackham, Neil, 105
rapport, *xiv*
reality testing, 54–56, 62–63, 102, 158
realness, 83
reciprocity, 52–53
recognition, 188–190, 193–194
relationship-building, 51–53
relevance, 83
repetition, 31
Reuven Bar-On Emotional Quotient
 Inventory (EQ-i), 5
Richardson, Curt, on giving back, 175
Rohn, John, on friends, 57
Rutigliano, Tony, 10

SAD (sales attention disorder), 18
sales, *xvi*, 21
sales attacks, 106
sales attention disorder (SAD), 18
sales challenges, 8–9
sales cultures, 160–178
 action steps for building, 176–179
 effective, 161–162
 effects of, 160–161
 generosity in, 162, 174–176
 learning processes in, 161–168, 177
 teamwork in, 162, 168–174
sales leadership, 179–197
 action steps for improving, 194–197
 best practices for, 192–194
 with consistent behavior, 180–183,
  193–195
 encouraging fun in, 191–192, 196–197
 teaching as element of, 183–186, 196
 with tough love, 186–190
sales managers, *see* sales leadership
sales meetings
 second, 95–97
 setting up, 119
sales pipelines, 154
sales results, 7–14
sales training, 44
Sanders, Tim, 83
Schledwitz, Tom, 76
second sales meetings, 95–97
Secrets of the Millionaire Mind (T. Harv
 Eker), 157–158
self-actualization, 14, 81, 82, 135, 161,
 162
self-awareness
 in agreeing and aligning, 117
 definition of, 15, 28
 diagnosing problems with, 72
 for discussing money matters, 146, 147
 in sales cultures, 162
 for sales leadership, 193
 of your relationship to money, 159
self-confidence, *xiv–xv*
self-improvement, 168
self-regard, 70, 72, 84–85
self-talk, 167

Seligman, Martin, 13
selling, leading vs., 194
"settlers," 81
short-term memory, 26
slowing down, *xix*
smartphones, 17–18, 32
Smith, Benson, 10
social responsibility, 14, 162, 169
soft skills, *xvii*
    for creating fans, 100
    importance of, 12–14
    for likeability, 69
    need for, 10
    for prospecting, 44
    for sales leadership, 180
Stead, Jerry, on learning, 164
Steady Relators, 129–131, 139
Stein, Steven, 11
stress, 56–58
success, 63–64, 183

teaching, 183–186, 196
teamwork, 162, 168–174, 183–184
Tear, Dave, on aligning words and
    actions, 62–63
technology-free zones, 17–18
This Is Your Brain on Music (Daniel
    Levitin), 37
"3Ws" sales approach, 108–111, 120
Toffler, Alvin, on learning, 165

tough love, 186–190
tracking systems, 114
training, *xiv, xv,* 44, *see also* learning
trust, 67
truth-seeking questions, 96, 195–196
truth telling, 27–28, 137, 140, 188

U.S. Air Force, 10

value
    analysis of, 103–104
    prospect's questioning of, 9
value proposition, 58–59
Varsity Spirit Corporation, *xvi*
vendor relationships, 88
visualization, 39–40

walking away, 151–153, 156
Walton, Sam, on appreciating others,
    178
Warren, Spencer, on decision making, 36
Welch, Jack, on leadership, 183
What It Takes To Be #1 (Vince
    Lombardi), 184–185
"what" questions, 109–110
A Whole New Mind (Daniel Pink), 10
"why" questions, 108
win-win approaches, 158
Wooden, John, on managing emotions,
    27